Baby, We Were Meant
for Each Other

Baby, We Were Meant for Each Other

IN PRAISE OF ADOPTION

Scott Simon

RANDOM HOUSE

NEW YORK

Published in the United States by Random House, an imprint of The Random House Publishing Group, a division of Random House, Inc., New York.

RANDOM HOUSE and colophon are registered trademarks of Random House, Inc.

Grateful acknowledgment is made to the following for permission to reprint previously published material:

Pink Martini/Heinz Records: Excerpt from "Hang On Little Tomato," lyrics by Patrick Abbey, China Forbes, and Thomas Lauderdale. Reprinted by permission of Pink Martini/Heinz Records.

The Producing Office and Paradigm: Excerpt from "Seasons of Love" by Jonathan Larson. Reprinted by permission.

LIBRARY OF CONGRESS CATALOGING-IN-PUBLICATION DATA
Simon, Scott.
Baby, we were meant for each other: in praise of adoption / Scott Simon.
p. cm.
ISBN 978-1-4000-6849-4
eBook ISBN 978-0-6796-0416-7
1. Adoption.   I. Title.
HV875.S565 2010
362.734—dc22   2010005887

Printed in the United States of America
on acid-free paper

www.atrandom.com

2 4 6 8 9 7 5 3 1

First Edition

Book design by Laurie Jewell

FOR CAROLINE,

ELISE, AND LINA,

MY LOVES, MY LIFE

Piglet sidled up to Pooh from behind.

"Pooh," he whispered.

"Yes, Piglet?"

"Nothing," said Piglet, taking Pooh's paw. "I just wanted to be sure of you."

—A. A. Milne, *The House at Pooh Corner*

Baby, We Were Meant
for Each Other

ADOPTION IS a miracle. I don't mean just that it's amazing, terrific, and a wonderful thing to do. I mean that it is, as the dictionary says, "a surprising and welcome event that is not explicable by natural or scientific laws and is therefore considered to be the work of divine agency."

My wife and I, not having had children in the traditional, Abraham-and-Sarah-begat manner, have learned to make jokes about the way we've had our family. ("Pregnant! Why would you do that? Those clothes! And you can't drink for months!") Jokes are sometimes the only sensible answer to some of the astoundingly impertinent questions people can ask, right in your children's faces. "How much did they cost? Are they healthy? You know, you hear stories. So why did you go overseas? Not enough kids here?" But we cannot imagine anything more remarkable and marvelous than having a stranger put into your arms who becomes, in minutes, your flesh, your blood: your life. There are times when the adoption process is exhausting and painful and makes you want to scream. But, I am told, so does childbirth.

We also know that the hardest parts are still ahead.

RAINDROPS RATTLED the roof of our small bus, seeped through the windows, and pitted the windshield with great wet gobs. "A sad day," sighed Julie from Utah, while the cityscape of Nanchang, China, slabs of brown and gray with wet laundry flapping, rolled by our windows. Five sets of strangers were together on the bus, about to share one of the most intimate moments of our lives. We had Cheerios, wipes, and diapers in our hands.

"A happy day," Julie added, "but also sad," and then we just listened to the ping of raindrops. A month before, this moment couldn't have happened fast enough. Now it was here; and we weren't ready.

We had endured three days of what we had come to call "adopto-tourism" together ("You will now visit the Pearl Museum and Gift Shop! Then the Great Wall and Gift Shop! Tomorrow, the Silk Museum—and Gift Shop!"), during which we talked about the sundry things strangers do to be companionable. "And what do you do? What kind of crib did you get? Aren't they impossible? Do you know that little Indian place just off Thirty-second?"

Over careful conversation between stops, we began to make some fair assumptions about the meandering paths of hope, frustration, and paperwork that all of us had navigated to get here. Most of us had probably tried to start families in the traditional manner. For one reason or another, the traditional result was not achieved. There are all kinds of wizardly things that can be done in laboratories these days; most of us had tried one or two. But wizardry does not always deliver. At some point, after all the intimate injections and intrusions, and the hopes that rise and deflate, many spouses look at each other across a field of figures scratched on the back of an envelope and ask, "Why are we doing this? There are already children in this world who need us right now. We sure need them."

A few weeks before, we had received a few photos in an envelope: a small girl with rosebud lips, quizzical eyebrows, and astonished eyes. She was about six months old at the time of the picture. A dossier prepared by Chinese adoption officials told us that she was smart, active, funny, hungry, energetic, and impatient (all of which remain a good description to this day). The officials had given her a name: Feng Jia-Mei.

A little girl named Excellent-Beautiful. From the Feng township.

We made copies of the photos, slipped them into our wallets, sent them around to friends and families, and doled them out like business cards, often to total strangers. "Jia-Mei Simon" was imprinted along the bottom, like the name under a photo in a class yearbook. Feng Jia-Mei, Jia-Mei. Excellent, Beautiful, Jia-Mei Simon.

Friends looked at her photo and wept. Something in her face, and in her tiny, tender shoulders, seemed to call out. We told people that the look of surprise in her eyes was because she had just read our dossier and said, "I thought you said that I was going to first-rate people!"

OUR SMALL BUS pulled up before a great gray file cabinet of a building in central Nanchang. So: this is where we are going to become parents. You walk into the building as a couple, and leave a few minutes later as a family. You walk in recollecting long romantic dinners, nights at the theater, and carefree vacations. You leave worrying about where to get diapers, milk, and Cheerios.

Grinning bureaucrats received us and showed us to a staircase. They took us down a flight and into a room. We saw smiling middle-aged women in white smocks holding babies, cooing, singing, and hefting them in their arms. We shucked raindrops from our shoes and coats. We checked cameras and cell phones. We looked at the women in the smocks and then realized—they held our children in their arms.

We saw Elise. She was five months older than in the picture we had, but still recognizably the little girl in the thumbnail portrait. Pouty little mouth, tiny, endearing little downy baby duck's head, fuzzy patch of hair, and amazed eyebrows, crying, steaming, red-faced, and bundled into a small, puffy pink coat. We blinked back tears and cleared our throats.

"Feng Jia-Mei?" we asked softly. The woman in the white smock looked down at a tag—as if checking the size—and smiled.

"Ah, yes. Feng Jia-Mei!"

She put her into my wife's arms. I tried to point a video camera, snap pictures, roll audio, and hug them, all at the same time. Our little girl's tears fell like soft, fat, furious little jewels down her face. As Caroline lifted her slightly from her lap to hold her, Elise soaked her own tufted little legs with a hot surge of pee. And then, as we laughed, cried, and hugged her even more fiercely, Feng Jia-Mei opened her small robin's mouth and burped up a geyser of phlegm, fear, and breakfast. Baby, baby, our baby.

Back in our hotel room, Caroline zipped, snipped, and unbuttoned four layers of Chinese clothing. Our daughter looked up into Caroline's unfamiliar face without warmth or disdain; one more stranger was handling her. First the puffy quilted pink coat came off. Then a black quilted coat. A mustard-colored crocheted sweater. A little red and white shirt. A tiny white T-shirt. Four pairs of pants, white, black, gray, and pink, each with a cunning little slit in the backside (among the greatest Chinese inventions since the compass and printing). And finally, pink socks that had been tucked beneath red socks: as tiny and dear as a kitten's paws. Each layer smelled of coal smoke and pee. We laid those small clothes aside to keep for the ages.

Shigu, our trip coordinator, came by our room. We told him that our daughter seemed inconsolable. Well, he had seen that several hundred times before.

"You should go downstairs," Shigu advised. "Get something to eat."

Our baby was famished. She inhaled a soft egg custard and plain white rice and stopped crying for a few moments, sobbing being hard to do while you are swallowing (though she tried, she tried). She sat in Caroline's lap, then mine. Her eyes were dull, defiant, and blistering. Her small cheeks burned so, I wondered if her tears would sizzle.

We looked at the other happy new families across the room. They smiled back wanly. They were having as much fun as we were.

I don't remember what we ate. Not much of whatever it was. I had a glass of wine, my wife had a beer, and we toasted our daughter. The drinks flashed through us like tap water. We ate and talked and tried to amuse, divert, and win over our daughter with songs, food, and funny voices, leaving her sullen and unmoved, all the while asking ourselves, "What have we done? What were we thinking? We've ripped a baby away from the only place she's ever known, to bring her some place on the other side of the world that might as well be the moon. What kind of people are we?"

We went back to our room. We called our respective parents, contriving to sound cheerful over our daughter's screams. We put her into her crib and stumbled across to the bed, kicking our shoes off like lead ankle weights, weary to the bone. We called over to Elise. "Goodnight, baby. Goodnight, Feng Jia-Mei. Goodnight, Elise Sylvie Jia-Mei Simon."

She just cried back.

We looked at the ceiling. We listened to the thrum of buses along the highway just outside our hotel window and turned our heads away from the leak of neon light around the edges of the curtains. It was no later than eight o'clock at night, and our limbs felt as sodden as logs.

"We love you, baby," we called softly. "We're glad you're here. We've been waiting for you, Feng Jia-Mei. We love you, Elise Jia-Mei Simon."

She cried, gurgled, and spat. We brought her into bed with us. She cried and kicked, cried and kicked. At one point I caught one of her little legs carefully in my hand. "Nice kick, baby," I told her, and sang, "All you really needed was the music, and the mirror . . ." She cried and kicked some more.

But after a while, her breathing changed gear, and she began to drift into sleep. We followed. My wife and I turned to each other across Elise's small, sweet, flushed, pink, teary face. Her small nose quivered three or four times with each breath. She kicked and twitched, but was letting herself fall into slumber. And in that moment of deep, condensed, and intense silence, Caroline and I realized that in the space of an afternoon, our lives had suddenly developed a few new and indisputable truths.

That my wife and I loved each other even more than we had a few hours ago. That we loved no one on earth more than this new, small, squalling, hungry, thirsty, and occasionally ornery human being that was now ours. Our baby had opened new chambers in our hearts.

And we realized: our daughter hated us.

MY WIFE AND I were up early the next morning, fitful, nervous, and sleepless. We took up positions on opposite sides of Elise and looked down as she stirred awake. *Our baby.* Elise looked to the left at Caroline. She looked to the right and saw me. Her face was blank. She might have been trying to remember the faces of her pursuers in a bad dream.

"We're on your side, baby," we told her. We began to chant, softly, "Feng Jia-Mei! Feng Jia-Mei! Feng Jia-Mei!"

She burst back into tears.

EXPERTS HAD cautioned us that children in cold orphanages were rarely bathed. It was just too much of a chore. So the first thing many new Western parents want to do is plop their child into a warm bath to wash off the soot of coal fires. But they warned that the babies, being unfamiliar with baths, will squall and claw like cornered cats. Wait, wait, wait, they counseled.

Yet it didn't feel right to leave our daughter to stew in her own juices after she had pooped, pissed, and whoopsied. So we drew warm water into a small plastic tub and plunked her in, along with a yellow plastic duck. She liked it, the warm water, the soft, fragrant soap, the rubbing, singing, and nonchalant touching. Elise began to splash; she smiled. We washed her gently and wrapped her lightly in a hotel towel.

And as she warmed up, Elise remembered to start crying again.

We placed her in the small, rocking Chinese hotel crib. She kept crying. We took her into our arms and onto our bed. She cried even more. Our love intensified with admiration. Elise Jia-Mei Simon wasn't going to fall for a couple of strangers just because we gave her dinner and a warm bath.

I HAVE A PICTURE I keep in whatever office I have and will ever have: my wife, a soft, raven beauty with a radiant smile, holding Elise aloft in her graceful hands, almost like a fluttering dove (I have made my wife smile occasionally; I have never made her smile like that even once). Elise is in a small white silk Chinese dress that we got—I wish we had a better story—at the Nanchang Wal-Mart, and she is also smiling. A grand, goofy, and mischievous smile that makes people smile back, laugh, and say, "What personality!" It is certainly a smile that discloses a hint of the charismatic and clever little girl she has become.

Because those smiles are so euphoric, and Elise's silk dress is immaculately white, like swaddling clothes, many people assume that it was taken at the moment she was placed in our lives. Actually, the photo was taken about three days later, after Elise had grown tired of crying and had learned that, however goofy and immature we were, the new people who had appeared in her life were easily manipulated into fetching egg custard, Cheerios, ice cream, whatever she wanted, whatever she wanted, *whatever she wanted,* whenever she so much as looked at us.

Our last morning in China, we awoke in the high-thread-count sheets of a classy hotel in Guangzhou. Elise was giggling in her crib by then. I wondered how a little girl from the wilds of rural China could wind up having a laugh that reminded me of Jerry Lewis. I whisked her down to the breakfast buffet. Smoked fish melted in her small mouth. Maple syrup dribbled down her chin. Our flight would leave in just a few hours. As we sat behind a huge glass pane overlooking the Pearl River, I traced the route that would take us from Hong Kong over Siberia, the North Pole, the snowy peaks of the Canadian Rockies, and finally the towers of Chicago. I promised her that soon she would see New York, London, and Paris. I promised her that soon she would ride a pony, dance ballet, see the cherry blossoms, and eat guacamole. I sang to our daughter:

> *Pearl River, wider than a mile,*
> *We're crossing you in style today.*

Elise spent eighteen of the twenty-one hours aloft snuggled and sleeping on her mother's shoulder. Business class travelers, who would ordinarily blanch on seeing a red-faced infant arrive in their premium-class precincts, put down their *Financial Times* and smiled; a few even gingerly chucked Elise's chin. On arrival in Chicago, we were directed into a holding area. We sat alongside families from Poland, Ethiopia, South Korea, Kenya, and El Salvador. No matter where their flights had begun, the small boys and girls had been dressed in pressed white shirts, dark suits, and plaid skirts to fly over oceans in the middle of the night and enter the United States.

An immigration official in a broad brown hat called out, "Simon family!" We smiled at the name, which we were just getting used to. He gave a last look at white forms separated by pink and green tissue papers. "Well, everything seems in order, Simons," he said, handing over the folder and pointing to a place in the customs hall about twenty feet ahead.

"When you cross that line," he said, "your little girl is a citizen of the United States." Then he put one of his huge hands gently under our daughter's chin and smiled.

"Welcome home, sweetheart," he told her.

A Short, Superficial History
of Adoption

ADOPTION IS almost as old as begetting. When disease, slaughter, or smiting felled, scattered, or incapacitated mothers and fathers, then aunts, uncles, friends, even total strangers—even enemies—often picked up and cared for the children left behind.

Just a few days after we brought Elise home, we went to Seder dinner at the home of my oldest boyhood friend, who is a rabbi. To hold in your lap a little girl who was left alongside a road in China while you listen to the story of a baby boy who was floated into the bulrushes alongside the Nile reminds you that the instinct to pick up and care for children is ancient; it may be inborn. But formal, legal adoption outside the family is a fairly modern innovation.

Ancient Rome had adoption. But it was usually a device to promote ties between wealthy, warring families and place male heirs in advantageous positions. Several Roman emperors, including Augustus Caesar Octavius, Constantius I, and Marcus Aurelius, were adopted sons.

Wars, famine, and village violence made orphans of a number of children. But most were taken in by families who made them slaves, not sons or daughters. Quite a few—boys as well as girls—were forced into lives as strumpets. There are still large areas of the world, China included, where this still seems to be true (and it is hard for my wife and me not to put the two small faces that we know best on that fact).

Still, there are some Roman legal records that suggest that a few families took in children whom they found and raised them alongside their other children, *as* children and full members of the family. They were called *alumni*.

Aristotle's parents died when he was a boy. He was brought up by a guardian named Proxenus, who sent him to Plato in Athens when he was eighteen.

Both of Leo Tolstoy's parents had died by the time he was nine. He was raised by a grandmother, who died; then an aunt, who also died; and finally another aunt.

In fact, if you ever wonder about the impact adoption has had on the world, stop to consider a few names: Moses, Aristotle, Tolstoy, John Lennon, Steve Jobs. And I don't even have to include Joseph adopting Jesus to make that point, though it is irresistible to add that Joseph and Mary had to go through a lot fewer interviews than my wife and I did. Well, maybe one major one.

The Catholic Church played a large role in bringing about modern adoption. The modern church receives a lot of criticism for adhering to family planning policies many believe only increase the number of abandoned children (and so they may; but people who believe that birth control will substantially reduce teenage pregnancies sound as naïve about the various reasons that young women have sex and get pregnant as the Church). But for centuries, the Church was also just about the only institution that offered practical help to scared young girls and their children. Young women left their babies on the steps of churches, and in front of nunneries, not to abandon them to a dubious fate, but because they knew that the Church would raise the babies they could not keep as oblations—gifts to God. The Church not only established orphanages and foundling homes but provided opportunities for the children reared there that often improved on the harsh class distinctions of the time.

Historians suggest that modern adoption in North America grew out of the great westward migration. Thousands of children got separated from their families in the push across the continent, for scores of reasons. William Tecumseh Sherman, for example, was born in Ohio, one of eleven children. His father died when he was nine and his mother was hard-pressed to care for her entire family alone; so a family friend, Thomas Ewing, brought him into his family. Other parents died trying to get out of czarist Russia, imperial Germany, or afflicted Ireland, or migrating from New York to Oklahoma. Their children would be taken in by fellow refugees or migrants. Or parents would work to get their children out with aunts, uncles, or family friends, and plan on coming over themselves within a few years; then Cossacks, Hussars, pitiless winters, or the czar's army would upend those plans. Stan Mikita, the great hockey player, was born Stanislav Gvoth, but was adopted when he was eight by an aunt and uncle because they could get out of Czechoslovakia and bring him into Canada.

Orphanages and foundling homes multiplied in major cities as children were abandoned, or simply fell off the sides of the engine of history. The Ruth family of Baltimore had seven children, but only two survived past infancy. The parents worked such long hours, for so little pay, that they signed their son, George, over to the custody of the priests at St. Mary's Industrial School for Boys. That's where Babe Ruth grew up and learned to play baseball. Some of the most principled social activists, such as Jane Addams, turned their attention to orphanages and foundling homes. So did lowlifes who saw them as sources of child labor.

In 1909 President Theodore Roosevelt convened the first White House Conference on the Care of Dependent Children, which called for the gradual replacement of orphanages and foundling homes with placement in families. Roosevelt called families "the highest and finest product of civilization" and insisted that children were entitled to nothing less.

I once did a story on the DNA studies that tied Sally Hemings's descendants into Thomas Jefferson's family line. I was not flabbergasted to learn that Mr. Jefferson had likely fathered one or more of her children. But it was fascinating to find out how DNA studies and oral histories suggest that a great many children in colonial society were fathered by someone other than the name listed on their birth certificate.

The fathers were not only slave masters, like Mr. Jefferson. Many children had biological fathers who were a family "friend" or neighbor, a traveling tradesman, a sympathetic parson, the spinet repairman, or a brother-in-law. As the poetry of Anne Bradstreet suggests, even Puritan society wasn't puritanical.

But I have grown to believe that while the identities of the actual biological fathers were often concealed, that doesn't mean they were unknown to their mothers—or, for that matter, unsuspected by the men who loved those children as their sons or daughters. I think many fathers just didn't care; they loved the child they held in their arms regardless. They chose to be their father.

This wasn't adoption, exactly. But it may have been a reasoned choice made by families who realized that conception could occur in an isolated moment of carelessness, naïveté, or duress as well as love. Real parenthood is earned.

Room Service, Please

WE RETURNED to Nanchang three years later. We had waited for another child for two years, and although I understand why adoption officials cannot say, "Hey, sure, take another," the second wait was even harder to endure. The day we were supposed to receive notice about when to go across to China and enrich our family with another child—we didn't. No one knew why. In the absence of hard facts, we assumed the worst. There must have been something squalid in our background. I must have made some public criticism of China that they couldn't abide. A neighbor must have tipped off Chinese officials that I spoiled Elise so much, they had to prohibit us from having a second daughter to damage with the love of an indulgent father who doesn't know the word "no" in any recognizable language.

Then one day we received Lina's picture in an email, and a notice that we had four days to leave to get her.

But first, the picture: a thumb-sized portrait of a chubby baby with red-apple cheeks sitting in a field of yellow flowers. "My gosh," I said to my wife, "it looks like Switzerland." (Photoshop Switzerland, apparently.) Paulina Luman Simon, named for my cousin Paula, who had just died, wore puffy pink knit pants pulled up to her chin.

"Like some guy on a New Jersey bowling team," said a friend.

Ten days later, we checked into the same hotel in Nanchang where we had stayed when Elise came into our lives (the same dismal espresso bar is on the ground floor; I made Elise climb into my lap and pose for a photo there, as I had when we first received her). Shigu, our trip coordinator, was with us once again.

"Be in your room at four o'clock," he said. "Your baby will be brought to you." I turned to Caroline and said, "Talk about room service."

We were too nervous to eat lunch, and merely picked at indecipherable items from the buffet. We inflicted Elise with stories about her first night at that same hotel restaurant— "Oh, you were so hungry! Oh, how you cried! Oh, you were sooo cute!"—and she was by now old and smart enough to sense how important they are for us to tell, so she indulged us as long as I took her in my arms for some ice cream. We went upstairs and read and colored with Elise, paced, stretched, and sighed. Four o'clock came without a knock; Caroline and I pretended not to notice. Then 4:05, and finally 4:10.

A knock at the door.

"My sister, my sister!" cried Elise. "Omigod, let's get the camera," Caroline replied with a credo for our times. We opened the door.

Two smiling orphanage officials had a baby in their arms. She was red-faced, she smiled gently, she was beautiful. They placed her in our arms softly, as if she were asleep. We brought her over to the living room table to put her down and take a look. Caroline blurted what was on both of our minds: "Are you sure she's the right one?"

The baby they had placed in our arms looked smaller than the one in the picture, even a little pale. She was hard to recognize without the Alpine meadow they had pasted in behind her.

Dire thoughts flashed in our minds. Had we been given the wrong baby? It's not that we were preoccupied with getting a child with certain qualities or lineage. We believed that any child given to us was the one meant to be ours. But we didn't want to fall in love with the child in front of us—she had begun to squall; we had begun to kiss and comfort her; the clock was already ticking—only to have the grinning orphanage officials return with sheepish smiles in a few minutes to say, "So sorry. Our mistake. Wrong baby. Hope that you didn't get too attached." We already had.

Caroline and I rolled our eyes up and down Paulina's tiny limbs, looking for clues while she kicked and cried. Then Elise reached out. She put her arms out to her new sister with a gentleness with which we had never seen her reach for a cookie, or our cat. She said softly, "It doesn't matter."

WHEN LINA WAS RESTIVE and distressed over the next few days, Elise was often the one to settle and comfort her. She'd put her own small hand on her sister's downy little head as if to say, "Look, our father is silly, but you can train him to do anything you want. And our mother is smart and beautiful. Don't worry. I'm your sister."

In those moments, the kind of platitudes that sophisticated people are usually embarrassed to utter suddenly looked as big, bright, and undeniable as the sun and moon. Race, blood, lineage, and nationality don't matter; they're just the way that small minds keep score. All that matters about blood is that it's warm and that it beats through a loving heart. I think that all parents want their children—we won't be around forever, after all—to be happy, strong, and brave.

But in that moment, Elise revealed something even more elusive and worthy: kindness.

I knew even then that our little girls would fuss and contend as they grow up. Elise was a sweet and exemplary older sister while we were in China. After we got home, she began to grasp that Lina was not just some higher form of souvenir but a baby who demanded scads of attention and heaps of food, soiled her diapers, and usually had to cling to her mother's arms. A few months followed in which Elise continued to hug Lina. But she sometimes embraced her, as a friend put it, "the way a python hugs a pig."

But at the moment when Elise saw a child enter her life in tears, the little girl who had once herself been given up reached out with instinctive tenderness.

Caroline took Paulina and Elise into the bedroom. The two grinning orphanage officials sat me down with a sheaf of forms. No words I ever put into an essay, news story, or novel will be as precious to me as the ones I wrote that will probably rest forever unread in the fathomless files of a vast bureaucracy.

"Why do you want to adopt this child?" the form asked. I answered, "Because we love our first daughter so much that we wanted to get her the best present in the world—a sister to come along for the ride."

MY WIFE AND I are still clearly in the rapture stage of parenthood. Friends—indeed, total strangers—observe the good times and abundant giggles that we share with our children and caution, "Wait until they're teenagers." They seem eager to teach us that the perfectly hatched chicks we hold in our arms have been wired with time bombs set to turn them into snarling demons when they strike thirteen. Parents often attach a story as a testament. "Cutest little kid in the world. Then the Hell's Angels rode through town, and . . ." I suppose that I have to defer to their experience. But right now, I enjoy the way our daughters reach out for life in bigger and bigger armfuls as they grow, and I look forward to those years, too.

(Show me that paragraph in a few years, on one of our worst days.)

So while this book begins with our personal story, I have also sought the advice of friends who were adopted, or have adopted (or both, in a couple of cases), and who have lived the miracle of adoption for longer than we have.

I have left out some names and details in some stories because everyone, including our children, will have to live with what's here, and I owe them consideration. But it's interesting that no one wants to leave out some of the most uncomfortable details when they know they are essential to understanding their story.

I also hope that I can earn a little understanding for my language. Writing about adoption is fraught with opportunities for people to take offense. If you write "is adopted" instead of "was adopted," or "foreign" rather than "international," some people consider it not just a verbal slip but a moral failure. I think that some of these rhetorical diktats make sense ("my child," not "my adopted child"). But several just bewilder and irritate me ("parent" as a verb) and even offend reality. Am I really supposed to say with a straight face that our daughters' birth mothers "chose an adoption plan" rather than "were forced to give up their babies"? And is any parent supposed to refer to those children with the Chinese adoption ministry newspeak term "abandoned" that fixes all blame for mothers' giving up their babies on the gallant young women who defied cruel edicts to bear them?

I don't think people write clearly when they're cringing. I hope readers accept that any verbal mistakes I make are committed with a decent heart.

OUR DAUGHTERS have always been told that they were adopted (the antique idea of keeping it a family secret to be revealed at some moment of maximum impact is, for obvious reasons, unavailable to us in any case). They know a fair number of the particulars already. They will learn more as their age demands, and discover as much as we do. Elise already knows a little about the chief alternative method for starting families (I'm thinking of pregnancy in the traditional manner here, not in vitro procedures; I have no doubt that one of her grade school pals will be happy to fill in the details).

But most children who have been adopted go through a

delightful period when they assume that adoption is the natural order of the universe.

(And indeed, if no other point stays with you from this book, I hope you will agree that it is.)

Elise once pointed to our cat, Leona, whom she calls Nana, and asked, "Mama, was Nana a baby cat in China?"

"No, darling," Caroline told her. "But she was adopted. Just like you."

Elise says that when she grows up, she wants to have a baby boy. "But China is too far," she said. "I think I'll go to Chicago."

Intimate Intrusions

THE IMPULSE to bear, as well as to care for, children is deep. My wife and I tried until we were black and blue from all the ways there are of getting pregnant these days, traditional and state-of-the-art. There are a lot of words to describe a couple who are trying to reproduce on demand. "Romantic" isn't among them. I will make no attempt here to describe my wife's experience, which was discouraging, depleting, and depressing. It is easier to talk about my own mostly comic aggravations.

You are invited to take a seat in the waiting room of a fertility doctor. Men nod tightly, smile wanly, and feign profound interest in an old *National Geographic* ("Clinging to life on an offshore crag, the nonmammalian tuatara has little changed its appearance since the Jurassic . . ."). You do *not* ask your seatmates, "And what brings you here?" When their name is called, you do *not* pump your fist and shout, "Go get 'em, tiger!" When your name is called, you do *not* smile, wink, and swagger out saying, "Back in a flash!"

An earnest young man takes you through a subdued hallway that looks less like a hospital passageway than a corridor in an airport motel. *Oh, if these walls could speak!* He shows you into a room outfitted with a recliner lounger, large-screen television, tissues, and piles of magazines that are not *National Geographic* (which might do the trick for a nonmammalian tuatara, but probably not for a human male). He hands you a small plastic cup. *No thanks, I never drink before six.* The nice young man asks if he can get you anything else to make you more comfortable. *Taco chips? A brewski? Hey, can I watch a ball game in here?* Poor choice of words . . .

He closes a door. You hurry to lock it. *Oh, sorry, sir! I thought Reproductive Services was the photocopier!* You hear the man slide some kind of sign into place. *Quiet—Man at Work?* You quickly survey the inventory of videos. *Where were these when I was a teenager?* Every video seems to have *Whips, Chains, Nymphs,* or *Studs* in the title, and I don't mean Terkel. *Frankly, my dear, I'd rather see* Casablanca. You leaf through the magazines. *Playboy* is on the top, but the interview inside with Quentin Tarantino distracts me. I admonish myself: *Bear down!* I pick up another magazine that makes *Playboy* look like *The Economist.* But the effect is not invigorating.

Finally, I lie back and think of England. The deed is done, the *Eagle* has landed, I came, I saw, I conquered (or perhaps that's in reverse). On my first occasion, I placed my contribution through a small revolving door designed to receive it (similar to the portal used to pass food to prisoners in solitary confinement, I noticed) and told a nurse, "I filled a couple of cups. In case you need extra." She sighed. "Every man makes that joke." Another time I was led into the chamber by a young medical technician who looked up from his clipboard.

"Hey," he said. "*The* Scott Simon?"

I nodded.

He called out as he closed the door, "Have a good day, Scott."

I wondered if doctors later looked at the contents of a vial under a microscope, observed the sperm kicking and swimming, and remarked, "You know, they don't look like he sounds."

Over the months that we submitted ourselves to such labored laboratory procedures, I'd occasionally have to cancel some kind of appearance. Of course, my small contribution was already on ice. The presence of the father at conception was strictly unnecessary. But the procedure was draining, mortifying, nerve-racking, and emotional. I wanted to be with my wife if it didn't work, and wanted to be with her if it did, and we could break out a bottle of . . . diet Dr Pepper. Public relations personnel would explain that I was having a "medical procedure." A few groups expressed suspicion. I was clearly healthy enough to be on the air. What kind of "medical procedure" kept me from fulfilling my obligation to them? The PR people hemmed, hawed, and finally said, "It's personal." *I'll say.* But ultimately I had to pick up the phone and tell someone who'd been especially persistent, "I'm sorry, but my wife and I are scheduled to conceive a child that day. I'd like to be around for it." He gulped and sent flowers.

I JOKE ABOUT all this now because it still hurts. If you are trying to create a child and can't, you feel that you are a failure. You feel that you have fallen short at one of the few things that scientists, creationists, Jesuits, Lubavitchers, atheists, polygamists, and monastic Buddhist monks agree that every living thing from a gnat to an elephant was put on this earth to do: seed new life. Continue the species. Keep creation *going.* Fifteen-year-old girls produce children with sixteen-year-old boys in the backseats of cars and in the stairwells of apartment buildings. Why can't two loving adults who have contemplated parenthood and are prepared to offer love, patience, and devotion come up with enough chromosomal matter to stick together and create a child?

You feel useless, worthless. You feel that somewhere deep inside your cells, you have betrayed and failed the person you love most.

You lower your drawers, give injections, jump at the jangle of the telephone, and wait for results. You wait for a miracle. A miracle was ahead. We just didn't know yet that it would take the form of two small girls who would be born to people we didn't know on the other side of the world.

MY WIFE AND I had talked about adoption during our whirlwind courtship. But it was one more dream on our list, along with seeing the Taj Mahal, living in Europe, and working in a Masai village.

We were going through some old framed office photos one day when we came upon one of me surrounded by laughing, smiling young boys, my arms outstretched to try to hold them all. It was a picture taken in an Ethiopian orphanage. I remembered that day—their blindingly bright smiles, their thin, soft arms as I hauled them onto my shoulders and held them to my chest, and most of all, the beautiful musical peal of their laughter. One of the orphanage officials said, "They're not used to someone loving them, picking them up and kissing them, almost like a mother." I went to sleep that night thinking of those boys. I felt them against my arms. I had always gotten on well with children (or at least seemed to amuse them), but it's safe to say that any parental instincts I had were invested in my cat.

Then I went to a party at a friend's house in Brooklyn, hit my head on the door getting out of the taxi, met Caroline Richard, and finally felt a love so huge it had to be shared, which I still think is the best reason to have children. When we got married a few weeks later, friends said, "But I thought *you* were the one that got conked in the head!"

ALL KINDS of adoptions are done today, in all kinds of ways. Expectant mothers can find lawyers who will look for a good family for the baby they know they do not want or cannot keep. This kind of private arrangement used to be done across town; today, it can almost as easily be worked out between a mother in Tashkent and a couple in Topeka. Couples can locate expectant young mothers and work out ways to take parental responsibility for the child they will bear that will keep the birth mother in their lives, too. There are women who bear children for other women, in which a formal adoption may or may not be part of the agreement, but some legal instrument is drafted to fix parental rights and obligations.

So many various technologies—communications and legal devices as much as fertility sciences—have created scores of new, cunning, complicated, and rewarding ways to have a family in addition to well-established agencies and programs. Caroline and I didn't weigh and reject them. But we'd been around the world, after all. My wife is French, so we were already a family of different nationalities. International adoption reflected where we had been, what we had done, what we learned, and who we were. I thought about the little boys in Ethiopia. I remembered sleeping on the streets to do stories about children who lived in roving bands in Rio and San Salvador, and all the little boys and girls in Kosovo, Calcutta, and Bangladesh whom I had held when they reached out, only to give them back. We weren't trying to do anything good—which meant that we also didn't reproach ourselves for not investigating domestic adoption more deeply. International adoption just seemed to *fit*.

So first, we looked into some areas of the world in which we had some personal experience, including Ethiopia, Bosnia, and India. Some programs were closed to us because of age (mine, to be sure, not my wife's). Others permitted adoption only in "special circumstances," which usually meant being the relative of an orphaned or abandoned child (covering the siege of Sarajevo and writing a novel about it didn't qualify). Some countries in which I'd covered conflicts—and this is good news—just didn't have substantial numbers of children available for adoption. Extended family members (and this is humbling) take children who are sometimes only distantly related into their lives.

We explored programs in other places, especially central Asia, that were known to have an abundance of orphaned children. But we got confusing information about the length of the wait, and we heard too many stories about families who had made multiple trips and paid manifold bribes only to be told, "The child that was supposed to be yours? There's been a delay. You'll have to come back . . ." We didn't mind slipping an envelope to some apparatchik with an open palm

(I am a Chicagoan, after all). But after all our frustrations in the lab, we couldn't bear the thought of making room in our hearts, then returning empty-armed.

Coming back from Amman once, I sat next to a UN official (Egyptian) who had recently been to orphanages in North Korea. His voice broke as he described seeing hundreds of frail, abandoned infants smiling and reaching up to him with matchstick arms. "You want to scoop all the children up," he said. "My wife and I want to adopt at least one little boy." Impulsively I told him, "So would my wife and I. No attention, no news story. We just want a child to love." We exchanged cards and embraces, but nothing worked out for either of us. Nor, as of this writing, for any of North Korea's orphans.

MY WIFE AND I had fallen in love in New York's Chinatown. Some nights, we'd trip home at dawn to the industrial a cappella of the iron grates over Chinatown shops being rolled up to reveal tiny, jam-packed storefronts, and see men in high boots bearing huge, bewhiskered, bug-eyed fish destined for tanks and crags of ice. Caroline led me by the hand through a twisting alley into a nondescript building that thrummed with the clack of mah-jongg tiles and the keening of Chinese opera. She had been to Shanghai on business and loved it. As a lover of great cities, I had learned a long time ago that if you need to find a restaurant, pharmacy, or grocery open late at night in New York, London, or Toronto, head to Chinatown.

We cherished the late night and early morning energy of Chinese places around the world.

Thus when we began to look into international adoption programs and got to China's, we stopped. There were millions of orphaned children (fifteen million, according to the current estimate) in China. The reasons were hideous. But the Chinese program seemed forthright, reliable, and—forgive me for putting it this way, it was reassuring at the time— businesslike. You met certain tests, paid fixed fees, and received a child within about a year, no spurious delays or hidden charges. You could trust that there would be a baby at the end of China's onerous process.

So we filled out forms. And more forms. Financial disclosure, credit history, medical, legal, and personal forms. You have to submit to a criminal background check, and while unseen bureaucrats spend weeks fussing in fusty old files (well, probably sleek new digitized ones) to ascertain that you are a stranger to them, your anxious, idle mind roams wildly. Could my name be among a hundred that an international drug kingpin, arsonist, or desperado maintains as an alias? Could the three books that I neglected to return to the Chicago Public Library in the eighth grade have accumulated enough daily fines to earn an arrest warrant for grand theft? That weekend in French Lick that I have a hard time remembering—could it be that . . . ?

We had to get letters of recommendation and found ourselves pondering which friends' names would be the most impressive. Politicians and press agents probably feel similar perplexities over endorsements. "Well, he's nice and all," you hear yourself saying. "But really, what does his name mean in Lijiang, Tianjin, or Chengdu?" You overhear yourself asking each other, "Don't we know some doctors? The Chinese *love* doctors. What about the one—oncologist, urologist, I forget—that we met someplace, remember?" Actors? Useless, unless we knew Jackie Chan. My oldest boyhood friend, the rabbi, might go over well in New York. But do rebbes rate in China? Another close friend is a Franciscan priest. Whoops— too close to a missionary. The Boxer Rebellion was not a protest by Muhammad Ali, after all. We have a lot of close friends who are journalists and writers. Journalists and writers? Not exactly high in the Chinese hierarchy, unless you count political prisoners. We have several close friends who are Chinese. But they weren't living in New York or Chicago because they were fans of the Chinese government (and besides, they had a discouraging habit of writing searing personal memoirs).

And then we were told that the Chinese distrusted Western journalists (come to think of it, so do I). We were told that they worried about Western journalists inserting themselves into the adoption network in order to travel around and see a different side of China. The thought that an American reporter would go through the stress, duress, and expense of adoption just to get some kind of inside story on China was, of course, preposterous. Still, on the advice of our adoption agency, they listed me as "Author of sports books." I hoped that we wouldn't get into an interview and have an official ask, "How 'bout those Jiangsu Hopestars?"

NO SINGLE HOOP that we were asked to jump through was onerous or ludicrous. Criminals should not adopt children. Neither should drug addicts, excessive drinkers, abusive spouses, louses, or tax cheats. But the overall effect of all the questions and tests can be oppressive, especially as months roll on without word of a child. Most of the documentation that you have to complete expires after twelve months, for reasons I respect (over the course of a year you can get sick, go broke, or get arrested). So when the wait that you were told might be six to nine months goes past twelve, you have to complete new forms (and pay new fees) all over again. *Grrr, grrr, grrr.* It's not the cost (though that pinches), or the time (though that grinds). After a while, it's the sheer galling indignity of being asked to prove, pay, and prove all over again that you're a worthy parent. Any true parent will tell you that that is impossible to prove in advance.

We had several interviews with a thoroughly nice and wise social worker. Those sessions were fine, even enriching. We posed for a "family picture," which naturally included our cat, Leona. Then our adoption agency told us that Chinese people do not consider cats to be pets (what do they consider them, God forbid—plat du jour?) and we should leave her out. We posed once more, careful to flick the cat hairs from our living room sofa.

Friends we have in China are puzzled and amused to learn that they do not consider cats to be pets. They own cats themselves. More telling yet: the first word that we heard from Elise when we brought her home was when she wiggled a small arm at Leona and said, "Mao! Mao!" I asked my wife, "How young do they start brainwashing these kids?" *Mao*, I soon learned, is Mandarin for "cat." It's a fair guess that Elise saw one or two in her foster home or orphanage.

We had to have fingerprints taken to clear our criminal records. I turn out to be afflicted with light fingerprints, a condition shared by about two percent of the population. The grooves and ridges of my finger pads are too light to satisfy the criterion for positive identification. (Oy. First, doctors question my sperm motility. Then light fingerprints. Will the humiliations never cease?) I kept returning to a grim third-floor office downtown to have another set of prints made, waiting my turn among a group of sullen parolees who had to do the same. As each new batch was rejected, my exasperation grew. "The Internal Revenue Service sure knows who I am," I pointed out. "They don't send back our checks uncashed and stamped, 'Who He?' "

During both our adoptions, we were seriously concerned that we might get the summons to travel but be unable to leave because of my undistinguishable digits (against all expectation, we light-fingered Americans are actually easier for law enforcement authorities to identify, because we are so few, which made our predicament seem especially silly). We asked members of Congress to intercede on our behalf with Homeland Security (they will do that for just about anybody). Each time, the FBI supplied a letter at the last moment, confirming that I was not (at least not yet) on their Most Wanted List.

All the conferences, forms, documents, and even expenses fill time, at least. What's hardest is the wait, and the months—or years—of what seems unfathomable delay. People ask, "What's up with your adoption?" You say you're just waiting. "But everything's okay, right?" You say you assume so. After hearing this two or three times, even good friends will say, "That's a long time. You know, maybe you should have . . ." followed by some friend-of-a-friend anecdote claiming that some fantastic bootleg scheme would have worked better than your naïve belief in observing the rules.

But worse were the associations and lists that posted reports that purported to explain what was going on. We heard that adoptions would be stopped, and we heard that they would be hastened. We heard that adoptions would resume in six weeks, in six months, and not for two years. We heard that China was so disgraced by all the stories in the Western press about the thousands of abandoned Chinese children adopted overseas that it would stop international adoptions before the Beijing Olympics. Or that the government would step them up before all the international media could arrive. It reminded me of the nervous talk among soldiers in the field who know nothing but have everything figured out. "Well, I heard from someone who has a friend who works at a bank in Dayton that does a lot of business in China that . . ."

To join these lists is to understand why the Internet has become both the greatest instrument for communication and the preeminent means of relaying misinformation in the history of the world. People who know nothing pass on misinformation and inferences to people who are so hungry for information that they prefer hearing nonsense to no news.

IN THE END I had only myself to blame if, after all the waiting and indignity, our adoption was not approved. We had Elise in our arms for our final interview with Chinese officials. A man on the other side of the desk sitting under the red flag with the yellow stars asked, "What kind of education will you give your daughter?"

I guess I had just grown weary of all the questions, the prying, the feeling like a pincushion for barbed official requests and an automated teller machine for agencies discovering another fee to be paid. Caroline says that I began to swagger before her very eyes, as if sitting up on a horse, tucking my reins and my rifle beneath my chin, and announcing, "Enough of this chitchat, hombres. We're taking our girl and getting out of this dusty one-horse town."

"She will have the best education we can give her," I told

the officials. I could hear my voice rising and tightening. I could feel cords knotting in my neck. "She will learn whatever she wants to and whatever she can. You see, she's going to be an American. She can be anything that she wants to be."

Caroline noticed the bureaucrats shifting in their seats as I delivered my Rooster Cogburn speech. She held up her hand to take over.

"She will be an architect or a ballet dancer," she told them, and they sat back and smiled with relief. They just wanted to know that we had a plan. French is the language of diplomacy, even when spoken in English.

There was one more moment to make us squirm. As we bent down to sign more sheaves of paperwork for Elise, an official praised the care children received in state orphanages and in foster homes. "Very fine people work for us," he said. "But every now and then we have a problem. Sometimes, one of the workers falls in love with a child. They will take the child and disappear in the middle of the night, and run off hundreds of miles away, because they do not want to give up that child." My wife and I stiffened as he leaned over.

"Don't worry," he cooed with reassurance. "We find them. We deal with them. We bring the children back."

Caroline and I muttered. Small grunts and rumblings to ask only each other, "And throw the poor people who love that child into a dungeon? Why not just let them be?"

Elise was in our arms. We would say nothing, including what we believed, to risk losing her.

IT IS·HARD to want to adopt just one child from China. Even the briefest glimpse of the vast scale of the adoption network, and the number of children languishing inside it, leaves you shaking your head and thinking, "We want another." That may be why the Chinese insist that you wait a year before applying to receive another child. A full year of sleepless nights, tantrums, and leaky diapers may be meant to burn away solely sentimental interest.

We were convinced that a sibling for Elise, and a second child for us (almost certainly another daughter), would apply the right amount of orbital gravity to all concerned. The wait for children from China had lengthened. But there was no question that we would return. We weren't trying to put together any kind of all-star team of children adopted from different datelines of distress, and we thought that two sisters from China could amplify and support each other for life. Parents can make only part of the journey with their children. We wanted each of our daughters to have a running mate through life.

The day after Paulina came into our lives, we went to the adoption center in Nanchang to fill out more paperwork and present ourselves to another committee, and then another. Caroline carried Lina in her arms. Elise wanted a little special attention and asked to ride on my shoulders. I scooped her up and settled her behind my neck. As we walked up the gray stone steps of the building, she sang a little song over the din

of car horns and bicycle bells in Nanchang traffic: "I'm . . .
riding on the shoulders . . . of our daddy!"

ANY PARENT'S CHRONICLE of their family will jump between times and stories, because every mother and father sees
their child in composite. In our eyes and hearts, they are several ages all at once. The headstrong teenager in front of us
gets all mixed up with the infant we used to carry and cuddle,
the grown, well-spoken father with the sniffling, babbling
tyke.

Our daughters can become brain surgeons, coal miners,
desperados, paratroopers, or prima ballerinas. But each time
I look at them some eye in my soul will see them ages six and
three, finger painting and giggling on our kitchen floor. No
doubt parents' view of their children is often sentimental and
deficient. But it's distinctly ours. We will remember their
nightmares and always see their innocence. We become their
advocates for life. The way we see our children as all ages at
once is part of how having children rewires our souls. It is the
special vision that makes us parents.

The stories I share from other families aren't meant to
prove anything in particular. Lives cannot be stamped like su-
permarket products, and adoptions cannot be graded. What
we take to be life's lessons are often obscure and inconsistent,
and they can change over time. But every adoption is, more or
less, a success because every child who is adopted embodies a
fresh new chance for the world.

Frank, Carol, Alex, and Scarlet

For Frank and Carol Deford, adoption was the only chance they had to expand their family. Their daughter, Alex, had died in January of 1980, after an eight-year battle from birth with cystic fibrosis. Alex was a luminous child, whose sweetness and ferocity as she faced death inspired those around her, and those who read about her in Frank's powerful 1983 memoir, *Alex: The Life of a Child*. Trying to have another biological child was out of the question for Carol and Frank. Though their oldest child, son Chris, was healthy, cystic fibrosis is hereditary. The risk that a third child would be born with it was too great.

Frank remembers that Carol suggested adoption early in the summer that followed Alex's death. He also recalls that he said yes with no joy in his heart, more to placate the wife that he cherished than from any wish to begin another intense and draining process when they had just lived through (*"barely lived through"* might be a better phrase) their most piercing loss.

"I thought it wouldn't work out anyway," he says today. "So I thought, 'Might as well humor her.' "

Frank was already in his mid-forties. While accomplished and prominent, he was certain that their ages would put them far down on any eligibility list. He asked his brother, Mac, for advice. Mac ran the Merrill Lynch office in Manila and knew a renowned local figure there named Marietta Santos. She told Mac that, in fact, she had learned of a fifteen-year-old who was about to give birth. But that baby had already been promised to a diplomat from a Muslim country. The baby was born on September 6, 1981, and when Marietta called the diplomat's wife to tell him that they had become parents, she asked, "What is it?"

"What is it?" Frank says she repeated.

"What is it—boy or girl?" And when she answered, "A beautiful baby girl," the ambassador's wife said, "Thanks, but we don't want it." Which is why to this day, Frank likes to tell people that if Scarlet had been a boy, he would be a Muslim living in Kuala Lumpur.

Marietta Santos phoned Mac Deford. "The Defords lost a girl, right?" she asked him. "Well, I have a baby for them." Scarlet was in Mac Deford's house in Manila within thirty-six hours of her birth.

And then four months of bureaucracy ensued . . .

IT WAS WHAT PROVED to be the last years of the Marcos regime, in the last months of martial law. There was no formal, legal, mandated program in the Philippines to assist and certify the adoption of Philippine children by foreign families, so bureaucrats sensed opportunity for corruption in all its beguiling forms. Carol, Frank, and Chris flew over bearing gratitude, finally expressing their appreciation to a court stenographer with a bottle of Johnny Walker Red. Baby Scarlet came back to Connecticut with Carol and Frank on a cracking cold January 22, 1981.

"Adoption is a miracle," says Frank. "I look back, and what are the odds? A million to one? My age. Our loss. A baby promised to someone else. In a country that didn't have overseas adoptions. And our daughter comes home—it must have been ten degrees below zero—one year to the day that we had buried Alex." He looks at his daughter across the room and smiles. She is in her late twenties, an artist, and has just been married. Scarlet shrugs teasingly and smiles back. "I mean," says Frank, "what are the odds?"

SCARLET DEFORD grew up in Connecticut as the only Filipina kid that she knew, or that other families knew (though her friend Meredith was adopted from Korea. America—where any little girl from any family can grow up with a name that could come from a tennis trophy at the Newport Yacht Club). Scarlet always knew that she was adopted; her visibly different appearance permitted no guesswork on that, even if Carol and Frank had been so inclined. ("But she has dimples like mine," Frank points out. "I assume they were there before we got her.")

Nowadays there would be workshops, encounter groups, and language and culture classes. But in the early 1980s, there was nothing to distract Scarlet from fitting in to her family's life with a minimum of analysis and evaluation. Carol and Frank, who are well-read people, read no books about being parents, or how to love, protect, and instruct their children. They didn't seek out support groups or associations. They didn't have the time, much less interest.

Frank traveled a lot, to cover Super Bowls and the World Series, give speeches, and profile Muhammad Ali (Frank Deford is, in my judgment, and not mine alone, the greatest sportswriter in America, and one of the best prose stylists in any form). But he also liked to take his family along. They went to Africa to see animals, and to Amsterdam to see Van Goghs. Scarlet went to many Mets games with her father and met all her favorite, cutest players (e.g. Ron Darling, now a team announcer). She worked at two Wimbledon tournaments with her father and met Pete Sampras and Tim Henman. She joined Frank at the 25th anniversary party for the *Sports Illustrated* swimsuit edition, and when a fan gave Elle Macpherson a bouquet of long-stemmed yellow roses, she handed them off to Scarlet. She says that she never dreamed of, idealized, or fantasized about the birth mother and father that she had never met.

(Indeed, as I read over the previous paragraph, I find myself fantasizing about being Carol and Frank Deford's child.)

Once, and perhaps, just once, Scarlet says she remembers a time when she thought that her adoption or race was being mocked. During the summer between seventh and eighth grades, she went to a ranch camp in Wyoming, where parents paid dearly for their Darien or Winnetka daughters with pink rooms and multifarious Barbies to ride horses, herd cows, and muck stables. A girl walked into their cabin, met Scarlet, and said, "What are you?"

"That set me back," she says now. "I hadn't heard anything like that before."

"What did you say?"

"I forget," says Scarlet. "Nothing. Nothing special. It was the only time it happened. I never thought that I was different from anyone else."

"Do you know what happened to the kid who said that?" Scarlet smiles.

"Oh. We wound up being friends. She was just talking."

"YOU WERE JUST so damn healthy," says Frank. "That was the thing. After all we'd been through. We were just so happy that you were healthy."

Alex's death from cystic fibrosis had seared and exhausted Carol and Frank. To hold your child as life slips away, and know that neither your love nor the latest genius of modern medical science can stop her from leaving . . . The pain is too terrible to contemplate or recollect.

"We were just so amazed—just felt so blessed—to see you so damn healthy," Frank keeps saying. They saw the little girl—one who nowadays might be classified and defined by experts as the daughter in a transracial adoption—as a little girl they were unabashedly delighted to see growing up in good health. They were relieved to have a daughter who could never be troubled by their genetic makeup.

Alex: The Life of a Child was published when Scarlet was two and a half. She grew up as a semipublic figure, not only Frank and Carol Deford's daughter but also the little girl who came into their family after the loss of a little girl whose life had inspired so many. The very first page of the bestseller says, "For Scarlet. So you will know Alex."

"I have to ask . . ." I begin.

"No," she says firmly. "I never felt that I was filling Alex's shoes. I always just felt very lucky to be here."

"Show him your tattoo," Frank suggests with a smile. Most fathers would not be so eager for their daughters to display tattoos. Scarlet lifts her sleeve to reveal a set of initials inscribed in lowercase script across her wrist: *f~c~a~c~s.*

Frank, Carol, Alex, Christian, and Scarlet.

"I always felt that Alex looked over me," she says. "As a child I remember having the feeling as if someone was in the room at night or following me down the hallways. I don't know if it was just a typical kid being scared of the dark and being alone. But when I look back now, I can believe it was Alex, checking out the new kid and watching over me."

THE DEFORDS went to the Philippines when Scarlet was fourteen, bringing along her friend Lindsay (another name that sounds like it's from a debutante's ball). As they came off the airplane, Scarlet turned to her parents and announced, "I'm in the majority now!"

When they went around town, strangers assumed that Lindsay was the daughter, and Scarlet her friend and traveling companion. But Scarlet made no effort to locate her birth mother or the suspected father, even though the redoubtable Marietta Santos would surely know something.

"If she was fifteen when I was born, she'd be married and have her own family then. I didn't want to disturb her," Scarlet says. "Besides, I never felt the need to look. If she's had other children, it would be interesting to see if I had other brothers and sisters . . ." Interesting, her voice suggests, but not urgent.

"When we were in the Philippines, you were what—five foot five and a half?" asked Frank.

"Tall as college guys," she confirms.

"And yet, when you were a little baby, you were the smallest. I guess that's environment," says Frank. He remembers that on their first night of their visit back, Marietta Santos organized a dinner to celebrate Scarlet's homecoming. "Jet lag, lost luggage, everything had happened," he said. "The mayor of Makati"—Manila's financial district, so inevitably described as the Manhattan of Manila—"cabinet ministers, everyone. We were exhausted. We were wrung out. They brought out this huge fish. They said she should eat the head." Frank shakes his own, and points at Scarlet, who was the guest of honor. "I have no idea how she did it."

As a young adult, Scarlet has lived in Jersey City, and met many Filipinos who are amused to speak to her in Tagalog, only to hear her reply, "Uh, oh, sorry. I just speak English."

"I'd like to go back to the Philippines for another visit someday," she says.

"Do you think," I say slowly, "that you might discover . . . something of yourself there?"

"I just think there's more I could learn," she says simply. "Everywhere."

"I guess we just weren't very good at all that," says Frank without conviction. He is talking to Scarlet, and turns away from me. "We just thought of you as this wonderful little kid who was whole. We never made a big deal out of being adopted. You were just a joy. And Chris!" Carol and Frank's first child, ten years older than Scarlet. "He'd gone through this absolutely awful experience of losing his only sister. Then, we dump this new sister on him. We were worried about him, some kind of breaking point. But he was great. Just great."

"More overprotective than *you*," Scarlet laughs.

"I can't ever remember a moment when you were growing up that I caught you crying," says Frank. "Sometimes, I thought you were so normal, you must be holding it back." Now he laughs. "I dunno—maybe you still are."

SCARLET FINALLY comes up with something.

"I had a conversation with a friend once," Scarlet volunteers. "I said to him that I wonder why I've always had one close girlfriend. Lindsay, or Meredith. But I never had a group I hung out with. You know, no *Sex and the City* pack of friends to go to lunch or dinner with and shop and talk. And my friend said, 'I know several people who are adopted, and it's the same story with them. Maybe you don't trust a lot of women because your mother gave you up.' "

Frank leans forward slightly, the tender father briefly supplanted by a curious journalist.

"If that's the case," he asks, "I wonder why you should be so friendly with the one girl? I mean, if the idea is that you don't trust women, because of what happened, if you were scared of something like that happening again, why would you always have the one close girlfriend? Wouldn't that be harder?"

We all look at each other and shrug—then laugh.

WHAT I HOPE I might learn from the Defords is that while adoption is a miracle, miracles finally take their places in our lives alongside more mundane things on our shelves and blend together. Adoption is a fact of life, not a trauma to overcome.

Carol and Frank had lost a daughter to an illness that had

lurked in their genes. They had a son who had to watch his little sister die. Frank asks, "Do you know how many marriages break up after a child has died? The mother and father can't depend on each other to pick each other up, because they're both sad about the same thing. They blame themselves, and then they don't know whom to blame. And you, this little thing, so healthy," he says, gesturing across the room to Scarlet. "I'm not saying that we would have broken up. I'm not saying, 'She saved us.' But Scarlet made us whole."

SCARLET TELLS ME later that her feelings about her family are so strong that she must hold herself back when she speaks of them. "Sometimes I am just overwhelmed with the feelings that I have in being so lucky and the loving people I have in my life," she says.

She is twenty-nine, a jewelry designer in New York, and recently married. (Marietta Santos left tropical Manila to fly to Connecticut in January, occupying the honored position of a grandmother in the wedding party). When her brother, Chris, got married just a few weeks later, Scarlet didn't ponder the toast she would give in advance, figuring she would walk around in some kind of puddle as thoughts and feelings overflowed. She trusted that something would come to her when she needed to speak. When the moment came, Scarlet cried so hard that she could barely form words. Friends and family were astonished to see the happy, composed girl that they knew overcome with emotion. A Deford unable to speak! As her father, Frank, had been at her wedding.

I take a chance on something with Scarlet: "Do you and your husband have plans for children?" She pauses.

"We'd love to have one of our own," she says. "And adopt one."

Frank sits back, a little winded. "You never told me that before," he says, then adds more softly, "That's nice."

"Just seeing how my own life has been changed," Scarlet says, turning to me. "To be able to offer that to someone else?" I don't think she means the safaris, Pete Sampras, and Elle Macpherson's roses.

Carol Deford, a trim, striking blond woman, returns home with shopping bags in her arms. There are kisses and kidding all around, crinkling bags, a shooshing faucet, and the bustling sounds of a family that has had dinner nine thousand times before beginning to prepare the nine thousand and first. They begin to gossip and laugh.

"I'm sorry that we're not more interesting," says Frank, as he slips a long arm around my shoulder at the door. But he's smiling gently, of course, at the preposterousness of what he's said. All the way to the elevator, I hear laughter from their door. I take the smile that they give me out into the street and all the way home to our daughters.

I OFTEN SPEAK with young people who say, "I want to get married, then adopt a whole bunch of kids who need love." I think that's lovely, and I encourage them. But I wonder how many of them follow through (my impression is—and the numbers would suggest—not many). Adoption is rewarding. But the process, as we have already detailed in some particulars, can be expensive, exhausting, and hard to sustain on a dream, much less a whim.

Children without homes don't need just people who are willing to love them. They need *parents*. Parents aren't simply good-hearted people who swoop in with hugs, candy, and promises. They are people who astonish even themselves with how gladly and rapidly they put their children at the center of their lives. Parents don't altogether stop trying to be cool, staying up late, or telling naughty jokes. But with their first cries, children call us to be less selfish and more humble (even humiliated). They give us a living stake in the world beyond our own short lives. Children reset our emotional and even biological clocks as we realize that they will, if we are blessed, live two, three, or more minutes for every one that we have left: we shouldn't squander a second.

At the same time, parents know that we would instantly throw all our remaining seconds in front of a speeding train if it would save our child.

I was sixteen when my father died. He was forty-eight, and drank himself into depression, then the grave. My grand-

mother was seventy-six and, because of crankiness and dotti-
ness, had come to be regarded by many as a ridiculous figure.
But when she stood over the casket of her middle-aged son
and cried out, "Oh, God, take me! Take me instead!" it was
the first time I'd really seen into the love of a parent, beating
in a fragile, noble, naked heart.

Parents are the kind of people who are enthralled and fas-
cinated, even as they are often exhausted and appalled, by the
challenges and vexations of children. There is no pretending
that picking snot out of a child's nose is as fun or rewarding
as making Halloween costumes. Mothers and fathers will get
angry and exasperated, will despair over a thousand irrita-
tions and affronts. But when their child throws himself or
herself on the floor, banging fists and spitting epithets, something inside a true parent smiles and says, "We can figure this
out."

Another Seat at the Table

For Jack and Pat Kiernan, adoption was a first choice,
not a last resort. It was a powerful instinct. Jack grew up in
his grandparents' house from about the age of seven after his
parents were smacked around a lot by life—health troubles,
emotional trials—and found it hard to make their children
their supreme priority. His mother's parents, Marty and
Marge Gallaher, saw trouble ahead for their grandson, too.

"They saw that the wheels were coming off the wagon," says Jack. "They scooped me up and said, 'You're coming with us tonight.' "

Jack didn't formally pack up and leave his mother's house on the north side of Chicago. Marty and Marge didn't apply for any kind of legal guardianship. He just began to spend more of the week at his grandparents' house, where the refrigerator was full, there was a quiet place to do homework and two adults who would listen to him, and he could be certain that he was bathed, fed, and had clean clothes. One day, Jack was writing a book report at their dining table when he realized, "Gee, all of my stuff is here."

When Jack and Pat met and fell in love, they began to talk about getting married and starting a family. Jack talked about his grandparents and the difference they had dared to make in his life. It sharpened their view of the kind of parents they wanted to be, which inspired Jack and Pat to think of adoption first.

"The way I had been raised had everything to do with it," says Jack. "To me, parents were two people who were in your corner when you needed them most." Jack and Pat, who were then reporters and had come to live in Atlanta, knew that there were troubled youngsters all around them who might be able to regain a grip on their lives if two people stepped in to them bearing care and kindness.

So Joey, now twenty, came to them from the foster care system when he was two. His birth mother used drugs and couldn't quit. His father was tall, Canadian, and nowhere to be found. Ian, now in his early twenties, was born into a family with drug and emotional problems and was passed through a succession of homes in the foster care system from the time that he was five. He came to Jack and Pat when he was ten. They had a son, John, in the traditional manner, and they thought their family held just about a full hand when they heard about a bright fourteen-year-old girl named Beatrice who had passed through group and foster homes and was currently bedeviling a nice older foster mother in Jackson, Georgia, who didn't quite know what to do with her. Jack and Pat were able to adopt their new daughter as she turned fifteen. And within just a few months, Bea was pregnant.

"Some days, I wanted to pull the hairs out of my head," says Jack, who now works for the American Automobile Association in Dallas. "But every day is different. Every day there's something memorable."

Jack and Pat Kiernan's sons and daughter didn't suffer insecurities from not knowing their birth parents. They knew their birth parents—and they were often their biggest problems. Joey, Ian, and Beatrice all came from households in which their parents took drugs and often drank, beat their spouses and/or their children, or let them go hungry with inattention and neglect.

"So Bea, Ian, and Joey have all had their challenges," says Jack. Of course, so have Bush and Kennedy kids. "It's tough enough growing up on the set of *Leave It to Beaver,*" he says. "Our kids were born into much tougher places. Nothing was ideal. And you know what? They're turning out to be wonderful adults."

He says that Beatrice, for example, has become a fine mother. "A *great* mother," Jack emphasizes. "She works hard and is doing the best she can. Children can look up to her." When Beatrice returned to complete high school while she worked, Jack was particularly proud.

"Single young mother in high school, everyone thinks they know about you. What kind of person you are. Do you know how hard that must be? I admire the hell out of her," says Jack. "The best we could do for each kid is to help them to learn from their own bumps and bruises, and all the shots life is going to throw at them. It's so great to see them grow up into nice young adults."

Which may be the most remarkable testament to the way lives can be turned around by adoption. Tough young kids who, in their early years, probably saw little reason to think that being nice earned any reward have become genuinely nice young men and women. And what I find best about the way that Jack Kiernan speaks of his children is that he directs credit to them, not to himself and Pat. He is a father who remembers how children, even when ringed by love, can feel ever alone.

JOEY HAS HAD drinking and drug problems, but he has been sober for four years. People who have never had to subdue that kind of beast clawing from inside may find it hard to grasp the fortitude it takes, hour by hour, to stay sober for a lifetime (which may be why Alcoholics Anonymous meetings are often more successful, over a longer period of time, than more expensive and exclusive addiction centers). Jack Kiernan says that his son Joey has developed that kind of character.

"He's a battler," says Jack. "He's struggled, he's fallen down, he's gotten back up. He's *battled* it. And I'm real proud of him."

A few years ago, Joey came out of thirty days at a treatment center near Houston and marked the occasion by going to a six o'clock Alcoholics Anonymous meeting in suburban Dallas. He carried his Lewisville Cardinals baseball jersey and cleats in a bag by his feet.

"I'm Joey, and I am an alcoholic."

"Hellooo, Joey."

When the meeting ended at seven, Jack Kiernan sped off for the local ballpark. Joey pulled on his uniform as Jack drove, fast. They got to the game in about the fourth inning. Joey's manager saw them pull up and signaled Joey: he was going in to pinch-hit.

Jack Kiernan was a young sports reporter when we met, and my godfather, Jack Brickhouse, loved him; Jack and I were among Uncle Jack's pallbearers. Jack Kiernan is the best ranking imitator of Jack Brickhouse's Wrigley Field home run call ("Back, back, hey-hey!"), and can re-create plays from thirty years ago ("Santo—to Beckert—to Banks—double play!").

But I have never known his voice to be so woolly with excitement as when he tells me what Joey did when he reached the plate:

"After about four, five pitches, the pitcher hung a curveball. Joey pounded a hard line drive over the third baseman's head. I tell you, it was a *screamer*. I don't think Ron Santo could have pulled it down. The ball hooked it into the corner, and Joey got a stand-up double. I'll *never* forget him standing at second with a big goofy smile on his face. I was fighting back tears. And not very well. I thought, 'This kid has gone down so many wrong roads. But now he's fought his way back onto the right one. God is looking out for this kid.' "

God and a couple of other people I can think of who are in his corner.

JACK WAS WORKING for an Atlanta television station and was embedded with a U.S. Army infantry division along the Iraq and Kuwait border a few years ago when he was able to cadge a few minutes on a satellite phone to call Pat and tell her that he thought he might be able to come home for the Christmas holidays.

"I have some interesting news, too," Pat told him. Jack

thought he was the one who was supposed to have interesting news.

"Beatrice," she told him. "Looks like she might be pregnant again."

"How did this happen?" Jack asked, and realized just as quickly that the answer to that was pretty obvious, even in the Christmas season.

"It was someone at school," Pat confirmed for him.

"I'll be home in ten days," he told her. "Sweetheart, we'll make this work. Whatever it takes, you know, we'll make this work."

Bea's sons—Jack and Pat's grandsons!—Bobby and Chuck are funny, playful, and smart. "We love them," says Jack. "They keep things light. Busy, but light. Can't imagine things without them. *Love* them."

Jack Kiernan is not a father who inserts the word "love" in every other sentence, the way some chefs will throw another pat of butter onto almost anything for richness. If you keep count, Jack says "flexibility" and "understanding" at least as often.

"Each kid came to us at a different stage in life," he says. "They had some heavy baggage they were carrying all alone. We tried to take some of that off their shoulders. You can't take it all, and not all at once. We don't compromise important principles. We have rules. But we try to understand the children we have and what's going on with them. We try to be flexible. We try to remember: as tough as it ever gets for us, imagine what it's like for them. I look back on my life when I was nine years old, lonely and unhappy, and living behind a taffy apple plant," he adds. "Now we're very happy, all of us, and I guarantee you, things are never lonely or dull around here."

Ian is about to go into the army. Joey is about to go to college, and plays baseball and hockey (hockey in Texas—do they make slap shots between the arms of a saguaro cactus?). And Beatrice—Bea has enlisted in the U.S. Navy. Do you think a young woman who made some mistakes but went back to finish high school while being a good mother to two young children might have some qualities of grit and drive that will motivate other young sailors, too?

Marty and Marge Gallaher are gone. Jack's mother is still a part of his life, in part because growing up with his grandparents let some of the sting out of his relationship with her. But not all. A few years ago, when Joey, Bea, and Ian were all going through touchy, risky, and demanding times, Jack says that his mother called and tossed off a remark like "Well, what can you expect when you adopt kids like that?"

Jack Kiernan didn't favor his mother with another sincere oration about the special joys of adoption, or about the singular satisfaction of helping children who need love to navigate the rocks and shoals of life. That would have been like reciting Pericles' funeral oration for her in its original dialect. And he did his mother the ample favor of not reminding her why he had wound up in his grandparents' house. Instead,

Jack Kiernan told his mother, "That's none of your goddamn business."

It must be gratifying to have learned enough about life to be able to tell that to your mother with such authority.

"IT'S KIND OF HARD not to say to yourself, 'What would their lives be like otherwise?' " says Jack. "I don't know. I don't think about that. As long as they know that at the end of the day, they have brought so much joy into our house. Even the stuff that's challenging. You get through it, and you all learn something. You all get better. You're reminded of what life is all about."

While Beatrice serves some of her tours of duty in the navy, Jack and Pat will be legal guardians for Bobby and Chuck (a legalism so that if either of them twists an ankle playing soccer, Jack and Pat can sign an approval for the school nurse to treat it). When Beatrice's boys join their thirteen-year-old son, John, the Kiernans will have a full house once again. Three boys: loud music, slamming doors, a packed pantry, and lines to get into the bathroom. Pat and Jack are exhilarated.

"I hope this doesn't end with Pat and me," he says. "Maybe one day, with their own families, our kids will look to find some child who really needs them. I mean, we've never said it out loud like that. But the thought might come to them quite naturally. I hope. Maybe they'll look around one night during dinner and say, 'Hey, you know, there's another seat at the table here.' "

Skin Deep

CAROLINE AND I went to several adoption agency presentations. Against all expectation, I was impressed by all of them. They often began with the announcement, "Everyone has heard a story or two about the couple that filled out all of their paperwork, paid their fees, and bingo—got pregnant." After the small, nervous laughs subsided, the person at the front of the room would say, "We've all heard those stories. But there is no correlation between filling out forms and getting pregnant. If you're here because you think adopting will somehow make you pregnant, you might want to leave during the break."

And I think a few people didn't come back after cookies and coffee.

Then someone else would say, "If you are adopting a child from China or Ethiopia, remember that you will become a multiracial family. Go home and ask yourself if you have a problem with that. Don't worry—we're not reporting anyone. We are not looking for a 'right' answer. We just have to be certain that you know what you're doing." I respected them all the more.

I HAVE ALWAYS been skeptical when someone proclaims, "I'm color-blind. I don't see race." For one thing, it seems to me the assertion is often made by someone who protests too much. For another, why boast about having limited vision? Race is part of who and what we are.

I know that our daughters are Chinese. I love who and what they are. They go to a class to sing songs in Mandarin, make dumplings, and observe holidays (and I thought Jews had a lot of holidays). However, whole weeks go by in which I may not see our girls as Chinese. For one thing, they are so many other things, too: American, French, tied into Catholic, Quaker, and Jewish families, and connected to Chicago, California, New York, and Normandy. For another—they're our daughters. I look at them and see stories, memories, and the way they can both put their hands behind their waist and strut like their mother (like Napoleon; or so I imagine).

Of course I know they are Chinese, and I don't want to act galled if someone innocently identifies them as such because it is written on their faces (I am still amused by ringside announcers who, in a match between a black and a white boxer, identify them by the color of their trunks). But while our daughters' ethnicity is one of the first labels that can be fixed on them, it does not account for and outweigh everything else that they are.

So far, I can count on one hand the number of outright racial remarks that we have overheard about our daughters. Those comments were so ridiculous, uttered by such obvious fools, that I felt it was more important to worry about our daughters' reaction (they had none) than to correct (a euphemism for clobber) the speaker.

Still, my wife and I have also felt that a few family members find our daughters endearing and adorable but not quite certifiably members of their family. (One elderly aunt recommended that we get our daughters the surgery to Europeanize their exquisite eyes. "Then they'd really look like your daughters," she said. "They really *are* our daughters," my wife reminded her.) Could race figure into their attitudes? For some people, maybe adoption itself takes some getting used to. We assume that in good time, the elemental kindness of all our family members will overtake whatever else they may feel.

I sometimes contemplate the day that some boor or outright bigot makes some kind of racial comment to our daughters that they will be old enough to understand. I hope I will be around to protect and console them. I also kind of hope I will not be there: I am quite sure that I could not be held responsible for my actions. I have tentatively decided that if and when this happens, it should be on the soccer field. Our daughter can shrug off the comment, turn around, and kick a goal. Then she can walk past her tormentor and say, "And you know what, buddy? I'm Jewish, too!"

For all the attention that transracial adoptions receive in the press, they amount to less than 10 percent of all adoptions. This figure includes international families such as ours, in which children from Asia, Africa, and Latin America are adopted into families that, statistics say, are predominantly white and heterosexual.

(And a lot of Jews. Caroline came home with our girls from their Sunday morning Chinese class one spring to report that there would be no Chinese class the next week. "Why?" I asked. "Because of the Jewish holidays," she replied. Wasn't it obvious? Only in America . . .)

Some of the most unfortunate thinking on transracial adoption traces back to a venerable source. In 1972, the National Association of Black Social Workers issued a famous statement detailing their opposition to transracial adoptions—"for any reason," they said, and continued:

We affirm the inviolable position of black children in black families where they belong physically, psychologically and culturally in order that they receive the total sense of themselves and develop a sound projection of their future.

Ethnicity is a way of life in these United States, and the world at large; a viable, sensitive, meaningful and legitimate societal construct. . . . Only a black family can transmit the emotional and sensitive subtleties of perception and reaction essential for a black child's survival in a racist society. Our society is distinctly black or white and characterized by white racism at every level. We repudiate the fallacious and fantasized reasoning of some that whites adopting black children will alter that basic character.

Special programming in learning to handle black

children's hair, learning black culture, "trying to become black," puts normal family activities in the form
of special family projects to accommodate the odd
member of the family. . . . These actions highlight the
unnatural character of transracial adoption.

These words sound archaic today—or worse. But there is
an ugly history that makes minorities (Jews included) intelli-
gently suspicious. Most of the ancestors of African American
families didn't sail past the Statue of Liberty but docked after
a murderous journey as slaves, not immigrants. America
wasn't the New World, brimming with opportunities, but a
killing ground of cotton fields and slave shacks. Aboriginal
children were once torn from their families and given to white
Australians. There were orphanages and mission schools in
America that saw it as their duty to rob Native American kids
of their identity and make them Christian. There are scandals
today in which infants from Ethiopia or Central America are
given to Western families in what seems to be a straight cash
deal.

I make no comparison, but I also try not to forget that my
parents were considered to have a "mixed marriage" in the
1950s. Six million Jews had just been murdered in the Holo-
caust, and many good people felt that those who survived
shouldn't dilute their number by marrying gentiles. A few
people in both our Irish and Jewish families felt, as strongly
as did the black social workers, that my mother and father

were foolishly heedless of the bigotry to which they would sentence their children in a racist society (it's an old story with bigotry—we say it's always someone else, not us, who harbors hatred).

But like so many millions of others these days, our family has become a mixture. Race is singular and immutable, but it's also merely one feature of our human makeup. I have covered too many wars all over the world to view ethnicity as "a viable, sensitive, meaningful and legitimate societal construct."

I don't believe that having an African American president and cabinet members, or having Hispanic, Jewish, and Asian judges, Nobel laureates, cabinet secretaries, movie stars and CEOs, absolves America of all racism or resolves for our children all the problems of bigotry and deprivation. But it is hard to say, straight-faced, "Our society is distinctly black or white and characterized by white racism at every level," when someone of Luo descent becomes president of the United States while ethnic strife makes that unthinkable in Kenya. Or when America is so plainly not just black and white but Hispanic, Asian, and all mixed up, too.

After years of controversy and refusal to change, today's National Association of Black Social Workers says that while they would prefer that African American youngsters be adopted by African American parents, they would rather see a child adopted into a loving home—of any race—than left to languish in a succession of foster homes. I don't know how many thousands of children might not have been adopted during the years when the NABSW policy was taken as definitive by many adoption officials. But I have a hard time believing that the place African Americans have gained in American and, for that matter, the world's culture would have been endangered if a few thousand African American youngsters had found families in transracial adoptions.

I want our daughters to remember that the first Chinese immigrants into the United States weren't doctors, engineers, Nobel laureates, or babysitting grad students, but indentured laborers who laid tracks and carved out mines in depths where no white man would deign to go. I want them to know that in 1882, after the United States had fought a civil war to end slavery, the U.S. Congress passed the Chinese Exclusion Act, and the burgeoning U.S. labor movement fighting for (white) workers' rights supported it (and that Canada, so often lauded for being more enlightened, passed their own obnoxious anti-Chinese law in 1923). And I want our daughters to know that there are still slave laborers today—in China. Probably not too far from where they were born or found. Kids that they used to eat congee with . . . well, it's too terrible to contemplate. But I also want them to know how history moves on.

ON THE TRIP on which we brought Elise home, there was another man in our hotel whom we never met but who earned our hatred. The same local adoption officials escorted him.

They told us that a baby had been selected for his family, but the man had come over alone because his wife was at home caring for their two other young children, who had also been adopted from China.

But when a new baby was put into his arms, he was appalled. "She's too dark," the agency said he had insisted. "She wouldn't fit in with our other children." He refused to keep the child. The agency briefly tried to persuade him that the baby they had selected was truly quite beautiful. But at some point, it became unwise to try to persuade a man to keep a baby he had rejected for the most heinous possible reason.

The adoption bureau kept all of his money (those are the terms, and everyone knows it). That baby, they assured us, would go to the next possible family—a better family. And that man and his wife would never be permitted to adopt a child again. We got the briefest glimpse of him being hustled into a car, to be driven to the airport and flown away. With our good riddance.

My wife and I eventually concluded that there was something suspicious about the man's story. His reasoning sounded dated, like Nellie Forbush's in *South Pacific* before she realized that her attitudes were uncool, even in the forties. Could a family that had already adopted two Chinese daughters be alarmed, much less surprised, at the complexion of a third? Some other reason must be at work. Had that man decided to leave his wife and children, and did he suddenly shrink from bringing home a child not to a whole family but one about to come apart?

We came to believe that for some reason we couldn't fathom, the man was so desperate not to adopt another child that he simply had to come up with the most hideous thing he could say to offend Chinese officials so they would send him away with no further appeals to decency. I wonder what he could possibly have said to his daughters who waited at home for him that wouldn't, in a decent world, get him sent to rot in hell.

EVERY STUDY seems to agree that children adopted internationally will have increasingly pointed questions about their origins as they grow up. That's not trauma. It's maturity.

The most extensive information right now seems to be about the several thousands of youngsters from Korea (KADs, short for "Korean adoptees," has become the term) who were adopted by American and European families, most of them white, from the early 1950s. One point the studies make is that the youngsters grew up as minorities not only in their communities but within their own families. They say that their parents surely loved them, but they didn't know what it was to be a minority. The Korean population in the United States was then relatively small; there were no workshops or culture classes for parents, children, or their blended families.

But when curiosity and the tug of discovery led some of the KADs to visit South Korea as adults, they discovered that many Koreans were chagrined to see them. Some people felt unvarnished shame that Korea had not cared for its own children. President Kim Dae Jung held a public meeting with thirty KADs from eight countries in 1998, to apologize. Many of the KADs matched stories about growing up hearing racial slurs in the West even as they went off to blue-ribbon colleges and rewarding careers. They recollected that their parents could console but not counsel them. What would they know about bigotry?

But then, South Koreans reminded KADs that one reason so many mixed-race children (typically an American GI father and Korean mother) had been sent overseas is that even in the time of Strom Thurmond, much of the United States was considered friendlier territory than Korea for a racially mixed child.

Caroline and I have always known that we have received our daughters because of a hairline crack in the great wall of Chinese history. On our first visit to Beijing, an art student took us to her studio (and gift shop!) and told us that she and her girlfriends sometimes wished that they could shrink into little balls the size of infants and go to the United States in the arms of adoring parents. In a few years, I think that students like her will more likely ask, "We spent billions of dollars to put on the Olympics, win gold medals, and dangle thousands

tle functional Mandarin while reminding our daughters that more than a billion people around the globe look like them (what's this "minority" nonsense?). My wife found several charming Chinese grad students. But given the busy schedule of their studies, we weren't getting out much. One day Caroline came home from a rare errand without our daughters in tow to find one of our Chinese scholars telling Elise to put away her Thomas the Tank Engine toys—in English. And why not? Telling her in Mandarin would draw only a blank stare. So why had we surveyed a three-state area for Chinese babysitters who were supposed to impart precious cultural insights in the language of their birth?

"Darling," I suggested, "I think we should stop racially profiling our babysitters."

And then we met Don-Don, a funny and effervescent young student from Shanghai who began to care for our daughters on rare movie nights. One night Elise asked her about her brothers and sisters. Don-Don told her gently that she had none.

"Most of us are single children," she said. "Our mothers can have only one child. You are so lucky to have a sister."

Don-Don said Elise reached for her hand.

"Maybe if you ask your parents," she told her, "they'll adopt a little sister for you."

Don-Don told us of the conversation that night. Elise told us the next day: for at least a moment, she was inspired to view her sister as an envied and valued gift, not a rival. And my wife—all right, I admit it, she was right—pointed out that Don-Don's observation would mean more to Elise for being uttered by someone who shared her birthplace. We may have missed a few nights out. But Don-Don gave Elise something enduring.

A FAMILY FRIEND once asked Caroline, "Do you feel guilty for taking your daughters away from their native culture?"

My wife responded courteously. I would have had a harder time. I occasionally feel rueful ("guilty" hardly applies) for ordering too much food for our daughters that goes to waste. Or buying them too much forgettable nonsense (that's a kind word, not the one that my wife uses) like souvenir key chains, odd candies (brown "moose turd" chocolate raisins from airport shops in the Northwest, pink "piggie pellets" candies from Iowa), and dancing hula girl pens from all over that I wind up crunching underfoot in our hallways in the middle of the night. I am personally embarrassed that I say I want our daughters to grow up to be happy and strong but, like a lot of fathers, I don't really want them to grow up at all. I regret, without guilt, that the mothers who gave birth to and loved our daughters, and risked punishment to leave them where they knew they would be found and cared for, could not keep them.

But we have adopted two real, modern little girls, not mere vessels of a culture. No doubt growing up with us will expose our daughters to all kinds of insidious influences of modern

Western life, from coarse music to vulgar materialism. But have you taken a look at China recently? Every Chinese child in China is gung-ho crazy to acquire those insidious Western influences.

Our daughters will be able to be as Chinese as they choose. Depending on their choices, that could take occasional special effort, including classes and trips. But my wife and I remember a young man we met while standing in the international security screening line at O'Hare to take the flight to China to bring Elise home. A Chinese American family from Kansas were there to see their son off for his junior year abroad.

"What part of China are you going to?" we asked.

"It's my year of foreign missionary work," he explained. He was a religious student. "Actually, I'm going to Kenya."

We were about to bring home a child from China who we prayed would never be victimized by assumptions made about the color of her skin—and we had already made assumptions about a young man based on the color of his. I was glad that our paperwork had already been stamped.

CHINESE PEOPLE—like Jews; like Indians; like Italians; like so many people who are moving around the globe now— have been growing up all over the world for centuries, from Aberdeen to Zanzibar. Our girls are part of that group, too. Chinese, yes, but also a whole lot of things. Our Chinese children sit at the Passover table and scrounge for Easter eggs.

They light candles in a menorah and write emails to Santa Claus. They march in Chicago's St. Patrick's Day parade on a blustery March day with green scarves around their necks that proclaim "South Side Irish." They speak French, like their mother, English, like their father, and phrases of Spanish and Yiddish that are the conversational buzz of urban America. My wife and I sing the Carrot Harvest song in Mandarin. *It's all in the family.* I think that transracial adoptions, like mixed marriages, don't shrink or starve a culture. They nourish it with newcomers.

Brown Eggs, White Eggs

ANNE, ED, AND TRAVIS BURKE are—all of them—prominent Chicagoans. Edward Burke is considered the most powerful member of the city council, a bred-in-the-bone, patronage-loving Chicago Democrat. Anne Burke is on the Illinois Supreme Court. But she did not become an attorney and judge (appointed, it is interesting to point out, by two Republican governors) until she had had the incomparable juridical preparation of being the mother of five children, four of them adopted.

Travis was born to a mother who was a drug addict. He came into the Burkes' lives after their other children were grown and Ed and Anne, who had been special counsel to the governor for Child Welfare Services, took children from troubled circumstances into their homes as emergency foster parents. Travis was eight days old. Years went by. Travis's birth mother struggled and never quite got hold of her life. He grew comfortable and happy in the Burke household because, as Anne says, "Every child in our family has different parents. And the same parents."

The Burkes undertook a long, bitter, public court battle to become Travis's legal guardians. A lot of people who didn't know Travis, his birth mother, or the kind of parents the Burkes are tried to score political points with the life of a real little boy who needed and deserved steadfast, dependable love more than bombast and rhetoric.

Travis is African American. If, outside of Chicago, you thought you knew that before reading the previous sentence, I'd gently suggest that many open-minded people who believe that they don't harbor biases do, and that the people whose thinking they assume to know may surprise them with who they actually are.

The Burkes took Travis to Africa so he could see where the ancestors on his mother's side came from in Cameroon. They have been to Birmingham and Selma, to march in memorial procession across the Edmund Pettus Bridge, so that Travis could see some of the hallowed grounds of the American civil rights movement and know it's part of *his* story as well as history. I cherish an image of the silvery alderman Edward M. Burke, who had (and enjoyed) so many blistering and colorful quarrels with Mayor Harold Washington, reddening in the searing sun of Cameroon and Alabama so that his son, Travis Burke, could know and esteem his African heritage. It is not a place or a role in which I would have ever envisaged Ed Burke—which shows both how little I really knew him, and how children totally rearrange our hearts.

Adoptions don't cut off children from learning about their culture (or, in our family's case, and millions more, *cultures*), lineage, or heritage. They widen the human stream that sustains heritage.

ANNE BURKE tells a nice little story. She had returned from a store with a dozen assorted brown and white eggs and brought Travis over to their kitchen counter to crack one of each into a bowl.

"See?" she said. "Brown eggs, white eggs, it doesn't matter. They're all the same inside." Then she held her son's hand against her own. "Just like people. Just like us. Brown skin, white skin, it doesn't matter. We're all the same inside."

Travis looked impatient, as if she were telling him something he had known all his life. Maybe he had.

"I *know*," he told her. "Arthur's father"—Arthur the PBS cartoon aardvark, whose father is a chef—"uses brown and white eggs all the time. It's no big deal."

We try metaphors on our children to make the truth into some more palatable parable of life. The man in the moon is there to watch over us in the dark of night. The Tooth Fairy rewards us for leaving pearls behind as we grow up. White eggs, brown eggs, yellow, red, blue, or green eggs, it doesn't matter—they all make a good omelet. You can even mix and match, like our family.

But children think in actualities, not metaphors. They lack subtlety and they lack pretense. They know that there are differences between them, and they show them off like their wiggly teeth. People come in different colors and it's no big deal.

Our daughters will know that race is a part of their identity. But it is only a part. A person's identity is established not just by what they are on the day they are born, but by what they become as they learn, try, and grow. Over the years, it's not just bigots who have disdained and distrusted racial progress, but people who have invested their careers and identities in race, too. I am glad that our daughters have come to live in a place in which experience and ability, not just ethnicity, can steer their lives.

Besides, I know that there is a much harder matter ahead for us to explain. Someday our girls will be at a picnic or swim party when we get together for a reunion with the other families who were with us when we got our daughters in China. Elise, Lina, Clara June, Jasmine, Polly, and Elizabeth will be at play, and we will tell them, for the millionth time, "Oh, I remember when you all were so small. I remember you all sitting on that same red couch when we got you."

What will we answer when one of our daughters asks, "How come almost all of us are girls?"

"How Come Almost All
of Us Are Girls?"

M Y WIFE, CAROLINE, should take over this section:

"Young children sometimes ask me what adoption means, and I find that I struggle to explain it. Because despite the reams of paperwork, obstacles worthy of a horse show, and a wait that can rival an elephant's gestation, adoption feels no different on the inside. I remember the first times the girls called 'Mama' in the dark of night when they were hungry, cold, or frightened. As I made my way to the crib, so touched by that word after the long, improbable wait, I thought, *that's it*. She is my baby, I am her mother, and it will always be so, no matter the complicating factors brought on by our unusual beginnings.

"To be a parent, according to Confucius, is to act like one.

"I AM GRATEFUL to my daughters for giving me the joy and responsibility of being a parent. And for reminding me how fragile the status of women is around the world. Our agency prepared us for all kinds of questions, like 'Why didn't you adopt domestically?' But the only indiscreet question I've been asked—several times—has been in small grocery stores by women who came from other parts of the world. 'Is this your daughter? Why doesn't she look like you?' When I replied, they said: 'Your husband allowed you?'

"There are many places in the world where a woman's role is to bear children: in fact, sons. In many places still, women who don't produce sons are thrown out of families, young girls undergo female genital mutilation so they will procreate for duty and not pleasure, and girl fetuses are aborted (the lucky ones, who end up in orphanages, are lucky only when they are adopted).

"In China, the imbalance in gender births due to the one-child policy is the highest in the world. This deficit in girls will cause further hardship for women in China, a country in which a significant number of women and children are already trafficked internally for forced marriage.

"It is difficult to track the number of women within countries who are victims of kidnapping, forced labor, and prostitution (though worldwide, victims are believed to be in the millions). Across borders, the U.S. State Department estimates that approximately 800,000 people are trafficked annually. Among those, about 80 percent are women and girls and up to half are minors. The majority of these victims are females trafficked into commercial sexual exploitation.

"It is one of the contradictions of our daughters' lives: given up by families who preferred to try again for sons and by a country who could do no better by them, they end up in loving families who wait years for the privilege of adopting them and in a country where they can be anything they want (except president, but that is due to their foreign birth, not their gender). There are no accidental adoptions, so no matter the early difficulties, these children know they are wanted and deeply desired. And in their adopted country, they can one day choose their careers, and they can have as many children as they want, or none, without being devalued as people.

"That is the other contradiction of our time. As women become prime ministers, secretaries of state, judges, senators, and surgeons, a staggering number are enslaved around the world, treated as property, or aborted before they have a chance at life. According to 2005 census data, 90 million women were estimated to be missing in seven Asian countries alone as a result of sex-selective abortion.

"We all know abstractly that our lives could have been different. In the case of adopted children and their parents, it is less an act of imagination to contemplate a different, less fortunate life. We believe our daughters' lives will be richer for understanding this.

"Today, there are tens of thousands of girls from China growing up in the West. The fullness of their lives will be a tribute not only to the too often underestimated value of girls, but also to the efforts of those who work in adoptions in China (including people in the government there) to ensure these children grow up in a place where they can fulfill their human potential. And bring great joy to all those who love them."

ALL OF WHICH is why I blubbered as we carried Elise over that line in Chicago's immigration port of entry and into the

United States. I may never be able to do anything else for her as important as that.

I am permanently grateful to China for the gift of our little girls. They will learn about Chinese history and genius, and know it is their own.

But it is impossible—it is irresponsible—to forget that our daughters are blessings that began with a crime when frightened mothers gave up the babies they loved because of Chinese policies that cause young girls to be cast away.

It is hard for us not to imagine young mothers who, in what should be a moment of sublime delight, sneak out to leave their infants (clean, warm, and well-fed) someplace where they know they will be quickly found. They hide across the street to wait and watch for strangers to take their child. When their baby cries, they must hold themselves back from rushing to them. Imagine the torture—really, no other word applies—of mothers who must watch their babies being swept out of their lives.

When you adopt a child from China, you face the fact that "a woman's right to choose" means abortion rights in North America and Western Europe. For a billion and a half people in China, there is no right for a woman to choose to *have* her baby. My wife and I didn't adopt daughters from China to make any kind of point. But the two people we cherish most are survivors of China's mass crime. That obliges us to speak out.

No matter the provocation of population, China's one-child policy is one of the great crimes of history. Over the last thirty years, the number of young women and babies who have been abused, abandoned, enslaved, or killed outright easily equals the millions murdered in other historic atrocities.

(The Chinese government has recently permitted certain minority groups—about 9 percent of the population—and farm families in which the firstborn is a daughter to apply to have a second child. I don't consider this a significant revision of a villainous program.)

The muted opposition among people, governments, groups, and international assemblies that consider themselves champions of human rights is shameful. Their silence has been purchased by China's economic power, and by a twisted political view that values sovereignty over humanity. Democracies flash an official frown at the Chinese government about human rights, then beg them for investments and loans.

The number of international adoptions the Chinese permit is tiny: eight thousand children a year, and getting smaller as the Chinese impose new restrictions on adoptions by people who are over fifty, single, gay, or being treated for an anxiety disorder (will this end all adoptions of Chinese children in Manhattan?). Yet an estimated 15 million children in China are left to neglect in orphanages—or worse.

I wish our daughters could grow up without knowing this. But that's irresponsible. My wife and I cannot read reports about children in China being dragooned into factory work or the sex trade and not think about what life might hold for two baby girls cast aside there. Someday, no doubt sooner than we would like, those thoughts will confound our daughters, too.

So we want them to know how much we admire the young Chinese mothers who chose to bear their babies even though they knew they couldn't keep them. My wife and I hope to give our daughters lives that are worthy of that sacrifice.

"Hang On to the Vine"

THOMAS LAUDERDALE says he's glad he was adopted. Not just grateful, though surely he is, to have been adopted by Kerby and Linda Lauderdale, but glad because being adopted just seems to fit.

"It suits who I am," he says. "I enjoy being some kind of 'mystery Asian' that fell out of the sky."

Thomas, in fact, is the adorable little boy giggling as his father thrusts him into the sky on the cover of his group Pink Martini's groundbreaking 2004 album, *Hang On Little Tomato*. The long, strong arms of the adult and the energetic unmuffled smile of the child all attest that it's a caring father lifting his carefree son above his head. I saw that cover for years before quite realizing that the child looks Asian, while the father looks white.

Thomas Lauderdale was born in Oakland, California, on July 14, 1970. He likes to refer to himself as a "mystery

Asian" and supposes that at least one of his birth parents was Japanese. His mother and father suggest that Thomas's origins are a little less mysterious (and less Japanese) than their son chooses to believe, but say they respect their son's right to know as much or as little as he decides. Kerby Lauderdale is quick—and proud—to note, "We just set Thomas on his feet, and have followed ever since."

When Thomas was two, his family moved to Indiana. His father was a Church of the Brethren minister, and Thomas would slide behind the church piano after services and find that he could pick out the melody of hymns that he had heard. His parents took that as a sign that they should buy an old upright piano, and Thomas has made music ever since. Kerby and Linda Sue Lauderdale adopted three more children in rapid succession after Thomas: Aaron, who is of mixed Iranian ancestry, and Jesse, who is African American, and Jennie, of mixed African American heritage.

The Church of the Brethren is a peace church, and it was an intense political time. But Kerby says that he and his wife weren't trying to make their convictions visible in the colors of their children. "We just didn't get Gerber babies," explains Linda. "And we had no problem with what they termed 'hard to place' kids. In fact, we welcomed that."

Kerby and Linda divorced in 1980, but they remain friends and committed parents. They moved to Portland, Oregon, together. Kerby came out of the closet and began to share his life with a man (Jeff Devore, who died in 1996).

Aaron and Jesse lived with Kerby and Jeff, and Thomas and Jennie with Linda, but only blocks away from one another, with the children running freely between the two homes. When Linda remarried, Kerby performed the ceremony. The Lauderdale family may have appeared unconventional, if not incomprehensible, to many outsiders. But Thomas, Linda, and Kerby say it all felt normal and whole inside, even though, as Kerby puts it somewhat elliptically, even for a minister, "the children were asked to do an awful lot of transitioning."

Thomas believes that his mother liked the idea of making a difference in children's lives more than she cared for the actual mundane mommy business of diapers, puke, and sippy-cups in the middle of the night. "She really wanted to be a cowgirl–adventurer–rodeo queen," he says. "That was perfect for me. I didn't want a lot of mothering. But my brothers and sister maybe needed more structure." Linda says, "Well, I did grow up on a farm," but is otherwise mystified and amused by the remark. "That's just the kind of entertaining thing Thomas likes to say."

Even Wynton Marsalis or Rahm Emanuel would find Thomas Lauderdale a hard sibling to follow. Thomas was always the smartest, funniest, most imaginative kid in town. He played several instruments, composed music, wrote poems, won symphony prizes, organized political events, and was a brilliant, entertaining speaker. Thomas was student body president and editorial director of his high school newspaper.

He went on to Harvard, where graduating cum laude with a degree in history and literature did not distract from his commitments as a party giver at Adams House, where he managed to slip in live orchestras, ice sculptures, and cross-dressing midnight swims (and where he met China Forbes, the dazzling singer with whom he formed the Pink Martini orchestra).

Kerby says that Thomas's multiple accomplishments may have fooled him and Linda into believing how much sheer love and care could steer the lives of their children.

"When you're handed an infant," he says slowly and painfully, "you think that you and your wife will have primary influence over that infant, that the child will be a product of your home. That turned out to be a dramatic misconception. I wonder now at our naïveté," he says.

"I grew up adored and beloved," Thomas explains, "with a whole group of adults paying attention to me. My sister didn't fare nearly as well. She never really found out what she was great at."

When Jennie entered her midteens, Thomas was already considered a civic treasure. His talent was his identity. But his sister felt that more of her identity might reside with her birth parents. Kerby and Linda discovered where they were living in the Midwest. They knew that Jennie's mother had a history of drug abuse and suffered from mental problems.

"But it was Jennie's right to see her," said Linda. "Her right to get to know them. It's every person's right." Jennie's birth mother, for that matter, welcomed the chance to meet her daughter.

"That bond between mother and child is important in both lives," Kerby says a little distantly. "There was always the question of why it was broken. And always a feeling with Jennie that maybe she could put it back together again."

Jennie told Thomas that for the first time, she could look at people and see reflections of herself, though she also told Thomas that she was startled to discover that her birth mother was white, with long, fair hair. Jennie's own self-image was African American.

Jennie became convinced that her background was a key to her identity in a way that Thomas's never was. Her birth mother was a real, frail, vulnerable human being who lacked a key to her own life, much less Jennie's; yet Jennie said that it made her aware of who she was. It filled something that was missing. Jennie began to spend several weeks a year with her birth parents. It was also about this time that Jennie began to use drugs. It is hard not to blame her birth parents, who had a history in that world. But youngsters scarcely need a family history of drug use to begin their own.

Jennie began to enter a spiral of drugs and depression. Kerby and Linda sought help and found support for Jennie. But she died in 2006 from mixing antidepressants and methadone. The details belong to her family. Linda says she's certain that the overdose was accidental. But she also knows it was the mistake of a daughter who seemed bent on self-destruction. It is the deepest, most grievous wound that a parent can suffer: a child who dies by her own hand. As parents, we are determined to protect our children from hunger, hurts, fires, and dragons. How can they harm themselves without our holding ourselves to blame?

"IF WE HAD had just one child, Linda and I would have felt we were much better parents than we were," says Kerby. "There is a human tendency to look for cause and effect. A lot of our sadness about Jennie turned into anger, and then we turned it on ourselves.

"Thomas always traced a lot of his success to the fact that he felt adored," he continues. "I think he would have been the same person in any family. Jennie was no less adored. But other things just overwhelmed her. Life is more complex than cause and effect. There are genetic, sociological, cultural things that just keep mixing up . . ." His voice trails off.

The pain of the loss that Kerby and Linda suffered may be sharper yet because it seems to upend the implied bargain of adoption: that we can give our children better, kinder lives than the ones they might have had without us.

I think that Jennie had such a life. The Lauderdales gave their daughter loving, reliable parents, a stable home, interesting siblings, and opportunities to break free from addiction. But as Kerby notes, life is not always cause and effect. There are always other factors and influences to infiltrate, frustrate, confuse, and distract. Drugs and self-destruction come into the best families despite the direct shots from goodness to happiness that we try to arrange.

At some point as you hear Jennie's story, you want to reach out to her with words Thomas wrote to the title song of *Hang On Little Tomato:*

> *Just hang on, hang on to the vine*
> *Stay on, soon you'll be divine*
> *If you start to cry, look up to the sky*
> *Something's coming up ahead*
> *To turn your tears to dew instead*

"In the end," says Kerby Lauderdale, "Linda and I tell ourselves that we don't deserve half the praise for Thomas that people give us. And we probably don't deserve half of the blame that we heaped on ourselves for what happened to Jennie."

Thomas despairs that his sister "never really found something she was great at." But Thomas Lauderdale didn't discover his identity: he devised it. He composes and performs songs in English, Spanish, Greek, Turkish, Italian, Arabic, and Portuguese, a repertoire Thomas calls "urban symphonic crossed with Cuban/Brazilian street Carnival parade, *Breakfast at Tiffany's* United Nations kind of thing."

"It's a relief" to have no knowledge about his birth or

birth parents. "It's more interesting," Thomas insists, "not to have any biological ties to the rest of the world. It's very liberating. I can be anything I want to be. I can be all the things I want to be." While workshops and therapies urge children who have been adopted to discover their identities, Thomas Lauderdale has created his own out of talent, ambition, dreams, and experience. I'm inclined to think that's what becoming an adult really means.

Today, Thomas is close to both of his parents and believes them when they say that notwithstanding what happened with his sister, they would accept and support his finding his birth parents. But right now, he says that he has no such interest. "Maybe later," he says. "Or when I hit fifty. But now, it's just great." Wherever Pink Martini performs, from Carnegie Hall to the Hollywood Bowl, the rows are filled with friends that Thomas has made along the way, from Indiana to Portland to Harvard and all their stops on tour. He gives parties wherever he goes, amasses friends, and exults in new enthusiasms.

But whenever Pink Martini plays Oakland, Thomas Lauderdale likes to end the set by announcing, "If there is anyone here tonight who gave birth to a baby boy here on July 14, 1970—come on back. We've got a lot to talk about!"

Adults Say the Darndest Things

THE PEOPLE we meet are nice to us almost without exception. But I don't want to be blind to the misconceptions and even outright prejudice that adopting families can encounter. Or perhaps I should say deaf. Caroline and I have both heard people say, right in front of us (sometimes right in front of our daughters), that someone they know (typically portrayed as the black sheep, knave, or ne'er-do-well of the family) is "not really their child, you know. He's adopted."

Breast milk enthusiasts are in their own category. They believe so fiercely in the power of mother's milk to enrich, nourish, uplift, and enlighten that they will corner you at parties to tell you that breast milk is the key to human development. "Why don't you tell the world?" they'll demand. *"Breast milk builds strong, healthy bodies, twelve different ways! B-r-e-a-s-t, breast milk makes the very best!"* A couple of times, when I've ventured gently to reply, "Well, we adopted our daughters. That just wasn't on tap," they seem oblivious to the offense it might cause parents to be instructed that our chance to do the best thing we ever can for our children was forfeited before we ever got them.

I want to be careful in flinging around a word like "prejudice." Certainly I prefer to blame my own stupid and insensitive beliefs on honorable ignorance. But families who have adopted are quick to pick up on language that reveals those people who claim to detect differences between birth children and children who are adopted. Of course there might be some differences; let's not be silly about that, or afraid to speak of them. But there are differences between birth siblings, too— just look at the Kennedys, the Bushes. No parent has exactly the same relationship with each child, by birth or adoption.

Most studies indicate that adoptive families are at least as strong as any other. In fact, the Early Childhood Longitudinal Study, sponsored by the U.S. Department of Education, the National Science Foundation, and the American Educational Research Association, suggests that parents who adopt may lavish more time and care on their children because they waited and worked for them. The study says, "adoptive parents enrich their children's lives to compensate for the lack of biological ties and the extra challenges of adoption." I wish they'd added "and extra pleasures" of adoption, but will add that here myself.

People who infer that somehow children who are adopted have less of a sense of identity or affinity with their parents ("not really their child, you know") may have it exactly backward. After all the bromides about bonding have cleared, the ties between parents and children in adopting families can be more intense. Maybe adoptive parents simply work harder because they feel that they cannot assume their child's reflexive love. Perhaps adoption lends perspective that sharpens and deepens what children and parents mean to each other.

Maybe it forces us to say what we are too scared and shy to state when it is easy, in more conventional families, for so much to be assumed.

But all of those are guesses. What we can report from our own experience is what Caroline calls "the extraordinary bond by adoption." Notice the preposition she chooses: not *of,* but *by* adoption: adoption is the agent performing the action. Adoption itself is the tie that binds.

"I Got Their History"

MAYBE THE MEASURE of a happy adoption isn't to strive for a child to feel no different from any other kid, but to turn that difference into a sense of purpose. Steve Inskeep was adopted when he was ten days old, and he felt that starting out a little differently in life conferred a distinction on him as he grew up in Carmel, Indiana.

Both of Steve's parents were teachers. Roland and Judy Inskeep had tried to start a family for ten years before seeking advice from their family minister, rather than a doctor, lawyer, or therapist, and they received Steve from the Children's Bureau of Central Indiana. Because Steve was considered (even by himself; especially by himself) as a smart-alecky little kid with a gap-toothed grin and a rangy gait, some of his friends looked at the map, sketched out some figures, and surmised: David Letterman was a student at Ball State in Muncie at the time Steve was born. Hmmm . . . The math, if not the facts, work out.

Steve is now an accomplished globe-roving broadcaster (cohost of NPR's *Morning Edition*), but he grew up snug and secure in Carmel. When his parents took the family to see a basketball game in Indianapolis (Roland Inskeep was also a coach), they would drive back home to Carmel the same night rather than stay in a large, strange city.

"We went all the way to Disney World for vacations," Steve recalls, "which was pretty sure to be clean and safe. But we never drove to New York or Chicago to see the sights. Those were the places we saw on television, with all the crime."

He sighs at the idea that being adopted was something to get over or recover from. But Steve volunteers that he availed himself of the peculiar celebrity of being adopted to explain any sharp edges: "I was always a little smart, flippant, and challenging. Some people would say, 'Clearly he's insecure.' Now I can't say it was because I knew I was adopted. But in any case, that was the story I had in my head. That was my plotline. But I was comfortable being the outsider, the stranger who has somewhat different attitudes than everyone else in town."

An outsider with a different attitude who tries to fit circumstances into a plotline. Steve Inskeep was becoming a journalist.

He remembers how he used to look at his face in the mirror. Steve's features are angular, handsome, and piercing, his eyes a cool greenish-blue. If someone suggested that he must be Scandinavian, you might detect it in his eyes or chin. If someone claimed to notice a strain of Chippewa or Iroquois in his sharp profile, you could see that, too. His ruddy, thatched head of hair? Scottish. Dutch. No, German.

"The thing is, in America, I could be one-eighth this, or a quarter that," Steve says. "You couldn't know my history, look at my face, and rule anything out. I rather liked that! And I think it made me more sympathetic to others who were a little different, too."

Right now, Steve knows nothing about his birth parents and says he is not especially curious about discovering them.

"If I got a phone call?" he says. "Well of course I'd return it. But . . ." Uncharacteristically, Steve lets the rest of his sentence fall away. He doesn't seem hurt or angry, just a courteous man who would return the call to be kind to a stranger who may need the emotional contact more than he does.

Steve and his wife, Carolee, have a daughter, Ava. They live down the block from two women who have adopted a daughter from Central America, and after they confided to Steve that they were eager for her to have a little contact with a sympathetic male role model (there should be a card for that kind of thing these days), Steve has found himself eager to oblige, and takes the little girl bike riding. He finds himself touched by the chance to connect and be of service to another outsider. It is tempting to credit that instinct to Steve's own adoption. And he seems to have used being adopted as some kind of spur and inspiration. But he also traces his character to the quality of kindness and the life of caring that he saw in and received from his parents.

Judy Inskeep was the first person in her family to go to college, and Roland was the child of rural schoolteachers who never had much in the way of wages or job security or saw much of the world beyond Indiana. Steve went to college at Kentucky's Morehead State because, he still jokes, "I thought that was as far away as I could get from home." Now he routinely jets between capitals and datelines.

Steve Inskeep sent me a note one day as he sat on a long bench to renew his passport. He says he always seems to wait until the last possible minute to renew his passport or driver's license, or receive a visa, and wonders if sometimes people who are adopted feel that, "Maybe, on some level, you are not absolutely sure you belong, not absolutely sure you have a right to be where you are."

But he doesn't forget the wonder of the life he has, and says that he is grateful to his parents for instilling that. They were not the kind of people to let good things go unappreciated.

"I confess that I'm kind of happy with who I am and the parents that I got," says Steve slowly. "I didn't get their genes. But I got their history."

ADOPTION RECORDS have been opened over the past generation. They were unbolted by the efforts of activists, often people who had been adopted and were outraged that the basic facts of their own lives were locked away from them.

But opening those files did not always occasion warm family get-togethers. No doubt a few seamy old family stories got dug up. Not every adoptive child, at sixteen or sixty, will be eager to learn about their birth parents, and certainly not necessarily eager for any reunion with someone who is, after all, a stranger. They may have been idealized; they may have been detested—most likely, a little of both—but almost always in a way that was distant and unreal. Feelings and priorities, though, may change from year to year as we grow older. We learn that the people we may want to meet may not last until we think we are ready to meet them.

Cherokee People, Cherokee Tribe

PAUL SIMON and his wife, Jean, were both members of the Illinois House of Representatives when they married in 1960 and began to have a family (I wonder if their courting could withstand today's ethics laws). They had a daughter, Sheila, and tried to have a second child. After a series of miscarriages, they decided on adoption; they specified that they would like a baby boy. Within a few months, they got a call from their minister. He'd learned of a healthy baby born to a teenage mother who decided that she could not keep him. Would Paul and Jean be interested? They were.

"One thing, Paul," said the minister. "I don't know how you and Jean would feel about this. The boy?"

"Yes?"

"He's American Indian."

Martin Simon has some of the same deep basso chuckle as his father as he tells the story.

"My father said, 'Well, that's just fine.' "

IT WAS THE 1960s. Paul and Jean didn't go to workshops or culture groups or take their son to Native American conclaves. But they treated their son's heritage with interest and respect. By the time Martin Simon was growing up in the 1970s, America had taken a turn. Native Americans were portrayed not only sympathetically but heroically in popular culture. Many children were more eager to be Indians than cowboys on the playground. Martin grew up with the Paul Revere and the Raiders song "Cherokee Reservation" ringing in his head, and walked around singing, "Cherokee people! Cherokee tribe!" He could feel the blood of great, shrewd, and dauntless Cherokee chiefs surging through his veins, and he identified with their noble, sad history.

When Martin became a teenager and had trouble raising a beard, he looked at his smooth, angular features in the mirror and found that they made him even more proud: he had the profile of a Cherokee warrior.

Paul Simon was elected to the U.S. Senate in 1984 and joined the Senate Committee on Indian Affairs. He attended hearings on reservations, and while he never pretended that he possessed extra knowledge because of his son, he acknowledged that it gave him an extra interest. In 1989, he signed a petition asking the University of Illinois to replace Chief Illiniwek as the official symbol and mascot of its sports teams (which, at length, it did, but only in 2007, after the NCAA had barred the university from postseason play if it didn't). *The Economist* wrote about the Chief Illiniwek controversy and gently noted that "Mr. Simon's adopted son is Native American."

As the Simons moved around between Troy, Springfield, and Carbondale, Illinois, and Washington, D.C., Martin says that he cannot recall being razzed by other children, either about being adopted or about being Native American. Which is not to say that he wasn't conscious of being both. When he felt anxious or alienated, he told himself that adoption must be at the heart of it. His parents loved him; he felt that. But there were empty spots in his heart that they couldn't fill; he felt that, too. Today, he believes that being adopted may actually have helped him sort through feelings of anxiety, identity, and the inadequacies of love as a cure-all.

"It gives you license," he says. "It lets you blame everything on one thing. Once you trace everything to that, other things become easier."

Martin says he can't recall ever wanting to run away from

home, and after a certain age, he ceased even to think about finding his birth family. He had learned enough about Native American communities in the United States to know that there was more likely to be a sad, depressing story surrounding his birth parents. He preferred the cool of being the great-great-great-grandson of an Indian chief.

MARTIN SIMON was twenty-eight years old, a White House news photographer, and living what he calls a carefree life when he picked up the phone one day and got a message from the woman who had given birth to him. Her name was Nikki. She had become pregnant ("in trouble" was the way it was phrased then) at the age of fifteen, when she was a student at an esteemed high school in one of Chicago's poshest suburbs. Her family hatched a plan for her to go away for seven months. Suburban teenagers sometimes took leaves from school in those days, to go into treatment programs for drugs, drinking, or anorexia nervosa—whatever people believed was deemed preferable to thinking that a smart young girl from a modern family had permitted herself to get pregnant.

Nikki had given birth to her son and handed him to a hospital nurse. In time, she met someone, and they married. But they didn't have children, and she didn't tell him that she had ever had a baby (Martin wonders now if she thought that this might have been somehow disloyal). Nikki thought of her son a lot over the years. But she held herself back from trying to contact him—even when she had a bout with cancer and worried that she might die without ever meeting her son—because she had read that adoptive children needed to be at least twenty-eight before they had absorbed enough of life to meet their birth mother and have a chance of grasping why she might have given them up for adoption.

Martin and Nikki talked on the phone—a long time. He had been reared by two compassionate parents, and he found himself touched by Nikki's story. And moved by her concern for the son she had never met, which had kept her away for so long. They made plans to meet in two weeks.

Martin took a breath and called his parents. Jean and Paul Simon said they were pleased, and a little breathless. Jean said, "Thank God this didn't happen when you were fourteen," which I translate as her thinking, *Thank God this is happening now, when you're already standing on your own two feet.* Parents who adopt, however well we have been prepared by books, workshops, and counseling to welcome such contact, and however grateful we are that our children have the chance to know those who gave birth to them, may forgive ourselves for harboring a lurking vulnerability. If and when we receive a call like that, we will be genuinely pleased for our child. But we may also grieve and gnash somewhere inside.

As Martin, who is now a father of two teenagers, says, "It's every parent's fear: If given the chance, will my children really want to leave me?"

It is impossible for a parent not to compose an unuttered

speech to their child: We reared you, supported you, changed your sopping, stinking diapers, caught your colds and coughs, and held your barfs and sneezes in our hands. We helped you memorize the multiplication table. We set a place at the table for you and laid your clothes out even when you were a teenager and told us we were witless, thoughtless, and personal embarrassments—and we never stopped loving you. We'll be god*damned* if someone who *gave you up* can just waltz into our lives when all the hard work is done and *walk away with your love,* like a woman who wins $50 million on a three-dollar lottery ticket. *Just* because you entered this world through her uterus!

There is also an instinct of parental protectiveness. These people hurt our baby once by not being there, even if they had good reasons. Who's to say that they won't finally meet them and hurt them again?

Nikki lived on the West Coast. She and Martin made arrangements to meet in Chicago. In two weeks, they found themselves circling each other, dazed with amazement, in the baggage claim area of O'Hare, detecting and delighting over similarities they could see in their faces, in the ways they stood, walked, and waved.

Nikki had light brown hair, like Martin's. She looked about as American Indian as Diana, Princess of Wales.

Hours later, after they had told their stories, swapped stories, laughed, and done a little crying for each other, Martin asked, "Are we . . . Indians?"

Nikki looked puzzled.

"It was on my birth certificate," he explained. "All these years, I've grown up thinking . . ."

"Oh, *that*," Nikki said, as something suddenly snapped into place. "At the hospital. They asked me to tick off some box. You know, white, Negro, Asian, whatever. And I said, 'Oh, we're all American.' "

THEY MADE PLANS to meet again in Washington, D.C., where Martin lived, and where Jean and Paul Simon lived, too, when the Senate was in session. Jean Simon told Martin how happy she was for him. Her words were warm, but Martin thought that they sounded a little brittle, a little unconvinced. Jean was a deft politician herself. She had applauded, saluted, and cheered for many candidates over the years who had shared a party line with her husband, and knew how to roar with zest for contenders she didn't know, and even louder for those she knew well enough to detest. Jean Simon knew when she had to make a good show. Paul had advised Martin, "Son, you're gonna have to be especially good to your mom for these next few weeks."

Nikki arrived at Martin's apartment first. They were having drinks and laughing a little too loudly when the doorbell rang. Jean and Paul Simon walked in, and Jean strode straight for Nikki. When Martin tells the story now, he has to stop, steady himself, clear his throat, and blink. Jean Simon walked up to the woman who gave birth to her son and hugged her.

"Nice to meet you, Nikki," she said and smiled. "Between the two of us, we sure created something pretty special, didn't we?"

"I'm so lucky," Martin says a little later. He and Nikki are good friends now, and even more. Not mother and son, exactly, but devoted friends with a place in each other's lives and a permanent stake in each other's happiness. Jean Simon died in 2000, Paul in 2003. Nikki, who is only fifteen years older than her son, has become a kind of older family member who knows him less well than an aunt or a cousin with whom he grew up, but is getting to know him better now.

Martin apologizes for having to stop and steady himself as he told the story, and has to hold himself back again.

"I'm sorry," he says finally. "But I really miss my mom." There is no doubt—none—about whom he means.

Our daughters stop traffic. Two winsome Chinese girls who speak English and French interchangeably as they chew bagels (or doughnuts, which they tellingly call "candy bagels"), turn heads, brighten eyes, and light up sullen faces on streets, in elevators, at restaurants, and in airports. People beckon us with cookies, smoothies, and big soft pretzels. "For the girls," they say. "My treat." Perhaps we should take our act into a BMW dealership.

Strangers and friends alike tell us that it's difficult to see our daughters laugh, giggle, and cavort without contemplating what their lives might have been like without us. Well, it's impossible (*unbearable* might be more accurate) for us to consider what our lives would have been like without them.

But we can't regard our daughters as rescued children. That would encourage us to treat our girls with pity, when we know that they're actually spoiled. I admit it. I am their spoiler-in-chief. We fathers cannot promise to forever protect our children from being hurt, sick, or sad. So we stuff them with food and shower them with things.

Consequently, our girls may yowl for jelly beans, but they are never truly hungry or cold. They have good shoes, clean clothes, their own rooms, more toys than FAO Schwarz, and four flavors of premium ice cream in the freezer. We live along a great river that is plied by boats and planes that bring the world to their door. They travel the world, ride horses, and take ballet. They have been dandled on some famous laps. Celebrities sign books and baseballs for them. When I take our daughters out to breakfast, if they so much as look at a bagel, bialy, cinnamon roll, croissant, muffin, or waffle, more food than a family of four would consume in many parts of the world goes onto their plates, and we walk away from the crumbs without a twinge.

Maybe I should be embarrassed. But does any father want his children to learn life the hard way?

Most luxurious of all in these times: their mother is at home for them.

We want our daughters to grasp the ways in which they

are privileged because we feel they will be better, stronger, and wiser for knowing that they have been cherished and favored. They are *not* victims. Their Chinese mothers loved them so much they risked prison by taking care to put them in places where they were sure to be found. Their mother and I love them so much we went to the other side of the world to get them. Our daughters might feel sorry for the parents who had to give them up. But not for themselves.

I KNOW THAT one day our daughters may be taunted about being adopted. Even as I sometimes tell myself that adoption has grown so commonplace that maybe they won't, I am reminded (usually by our daughters themselves) how children can be as fiendish and scheming as Stasi agents. So of course Elise and Lina will be teased about being adopted. And they will tease other children for being curly-haired or freckled. Kids toss whatever crockery is around. They will also be teased for being Chinese, French, Jewish, or left-handed, and for wearing their hair, as their mother likes them to right now, in adorable little French braids. But they will grow up knowing that they should be only proud about being adopted. I will consider it a parental failure if our daughters ever try to use it as some kind of excuse.

But I don't want my determination to make me willfully blind to features of their personalities that may be tied up with the way they came into our lives. I don't want my eagerness to believe that adoption makes no difference in the way a child is loved—or even, as I am convinced, that it makes only a positive difference—to make me insensitive to the ways in which our daughters may need our support.

A Primal Wound?

IT IS NOT POSSIBLE to talk about modern adoption without considering Nancy Verrier. Her 1993 book *The Primal Wound: Understanding the Adopted Child* is an eloquent argument, written both from her personal experience as a psychotherapist and from her heart as the mother of two children she has adopted. Thousands of people who have been adopted cite her work as the missing piece of their lives that has at last made happiness possible. In her clinical work, writing, and teaching she no doubt does more good for more people in a single month than I have in my lifetime.

You can tell that a big fat "but" is ahead.

NANCY VERRIER believes that a "primal wound" is inflicted whenever a mother and child are separated, and that this is true of children who leave their mother's side just after birth or months or years thereafter. She believes that this primal wound is physical—cellular and structural as well as emotional and spiritual—and that the pain of detachment for mother and child persists, even if people profess not to remember it. This primal wound is unavoidable, and impossible for either mother or child to recover from fully. The wound endures. Love helps, but it is not a cure. The primal wound is not some boo-boo that can be kissed away or healed by ice cream and pony rides.

Nancy Verrier says:

This wound, occurring before the child has begun to separate his own identity from that of the mother, is experienced not only as a loss of the mother, but as a loss of the Self, that core-being of oneself which is the center of goodness and wholeness. The child may be left with a sense that part of oneself has disappeared, a feeling of incompleteness, a lack of wholeness. In addition to the genealogical sense of being cut off from one's roots, this incompleteness is often experienced in a physical sense of bodily incompleteness, a hurt from something missing.

This is rough stuff for parents to read. It suggests that, love notwithstanding, nothing we have done or can do can spare our children persisting pain. Our pride in the difference that our own care and love may make can prevent us from seeing this wound.

It is hard for parents to hear her analysis and not think we have been accused of ignoring some great brutality toward the persons we love most.

"Babies know their mothers," Nancy Verrier told me. She is a gracious woman who is used to receiving skeptical calls from parents—and writers—like me, and has a therapist's gift for phrasing advice in the way that disarms suspicion.

"The babies know their mother's voice, their heartbeat, their smell, their skin. When they get adopted, they know that the person holding them is not that same person. It's disconcerting. Mom is everything to them. It destroys their whole world. There are lots of things that get delayed—the whole post-natal bonding period that should follow. That important bond is severed. It's pretty terrifying, actually. I believe in adoption. But we have to be realistic. They (the children) start life severed from the world they know."

It is easy to flippantly dismiss what Nancy Verrier says. Believe me, I have ("Well, I think I suffered a primal wound when I wasn't born as Warren Buffett's son"). But I try to listen because she also advises—and here, I am more impressed by her practical experience as a therapist than her career as a theorizer—that "the children who feel most connected to their adoptive parents are the ones whose parents truly understand their loss. . . . Their loss is hard to see. Children don't grieve the same way adults do. You have to know what to look for."

Andrew's Family

"I THINK THAT childbirth is often revered in memory," says Steve Levitt, the University of Chicago economist and best-selling author. "But not the real experience. It gets idealized later." He has more right—more experience—than most men to make that observation. And Steve and his wife, Jeanette, certainly suffered a primal wound.

Their son Andrew was just a year old when he came down with a slight fever. He died in a hospital just a few days later, from rare and incurable pneumococcal meningitis. Steve and Jeanette started going to a support group for grieving parents, and they noticed how many children had died in swimming pool accidents. Steve was already beginning to try to apply his economist's perception to broader events, and he discovered some startling statistics.

Every year, one child dies for every 11,000 swimming pools. But roughly one child dies from a gunshot for every one million guns. So Steve wrote a short, shocking piece for the *Chicago Sun-Times* that began, "If you own a gun and have a swimming pool in the yard, the swimming pool is almost 100 times more likely to kill a child than the gun is."

He didn't imply that guns were household toys but rather that backyard swimming pools were significantly more dangerous than people realized. It was the beginning of a whole new analytical approach that resulted in Steve's bestselling 2005 book, *Freakonomics: A Rogue Economist Explores the Hidden Side of Everything,* and a 2009 sequel, *Superfreakonomics.*

As Steve took the chance to learn something, anything, from his grief, he and Jeanette decided to adopt a child from China. Conceiving their first child had been difficult. They were emotionally fragile. "Chinese adoption was simple," he explains. "There was a direct list of steps to get a child, as opposed to domestic adoption or other ways that had no guarantees."

And then Jeanette Levitt got pregnant. They welcomed a daughter, Olivia, who was eleven months old when Steve and Jeanette received their thumbnail-size photo of the daughter in China who was waiting for them. Jeanette had to stay in Chicago with their baby, and Steve went to China.

"When we first got Amanda's picture," he said, "it was the strangest thing. She was just the most beautiful baby that I had ever seen. When I went to China for her, it was instantaneous. By the end of the first day I had fallen completely in love with her. By the end of this trip my bond with her was stronger that I have ever had with any other human being—with my other children, with my wife. Stronger than the bond I had when I was a baby with my parents. I really chalk it up to my chance to be a mother as opposed to a father. Because my wife wasn't there, because it was my responsibility to take care of her. And she was nine months old, so she was ready to have a mother. I had never been a mother, and she had never had one. It was just incredibly powerful.

"We had just lost a child we loved," Steve softly recalls. "Then, we had a daughter that we loved. Then Amanda, put into my hands. I never predicted that I would be able to love this 'stranger' so quickly, but I did. It changed the way I thought about genes, nature versus nurture, and the way we are wired to love our children. We are set up to love children, and make them ours."

Steve and Jeanette now have four children. Olivia and Amanda are eight. Nicholas, a biological son, is six, and Sophie, who is five, is also adopted from China. Steve says that every few months he tries to talk to Amanda about the circumstances of her birth in China, and how and why young mothers may cast away daughters that they love.

"I have talked to my daughter as an economist about this issue," he says. One imagines the winner of the John Bates Clark medal in economics at his daughter's bedside, pointing at pie charts among the stuffed bunnies and princess dolls. "And so far, she couldn't be less interested. She's like, 'Okay, now let's talk about something that's more interesting.' " Someday the topic may be of more interest to Amanda, and may she remember that her father always thought it was.

STEVE LEVITT is skeptical that children who are adopted suffer a wound that endures. "I'm sure that a lot of people, adopted and not adopted, would like to pin all of their problems of happiness or uncertainty on having a primal wound," he says. "It makes everything fit so nicely. I can see why a lot of people say, 'That explains a lot about why I feel the way I do.' But the brains of young children don't function like that. Let me give you an example.

"Within two days of meeting my daughter Amanda, we had a reunion with her caretakers. She didn't show the slightest bit of interest in them. She was just totally bonded to me. Those were the people who took care of her for the first nine months, and as far as she was concerned, they had been her parents. But when she found someone new who was totally devoted to her one hundred percent, she just said, 'Forget you.' "

Steve Levitt notes, with academic respect, that he is not a psychologist. But he needs little instruction about how human beings get through grief. He believes that infants possess astoundingly supple minds. Their neurons absorb a thousand new things every day, and get rid of, or learn how to disregard, what they don't need so they can keep going. We may not forget, but we know it's important to go on. The millions of things that we know or feel (or think we do) get sorted by some electrical impulse of survival. That spark puts what needs to be on top so that we can move on.

STEVE POSTS a small entry on his website every year on the anniversary of Andrew's death in October. "He was born just as the leaves were turning," he says. "And he died just as the leaves were turning."

Like Frank and Carol Deford, Steve and Jeanette Levitt have made the son they lost a member of the family they have become. All of their children will know of him, and they will know that however their own lives began, Andrew's enlivens them. Steve reminds friends of the song from *Rent* they played at Andrew's memorial. Their little boy had just a year on this earth and in their lives. But the economist whose own distinct view of data has redefined so many important public debates reminds us that the lifetime joys of children don't have a measurable index. He thinks of the year that was Andrew's life:

525,600 minutes,

525,600 moments so dear,

525,600 minutes—how do you measure, measure a year?

In daylights, in sunsets, in midnights, in cups of coffee,

In inches, in miles, in laughter, in strife.

In 525,600 minutes—how do you measure a year in the life?

How about love? How about love? How about love?

THOSE OF US who adopt get dazzled when we begin to see some of our own traits in our children. I swear that I can hear my father's laugh in our two daughters. Steve Levitt was touched to come to a parent-teacher conference at Amanda's kindergarten and be told that she seemed good with numbers and gifted with the power of critical thinking (our daughters have those traits, too; I have often heard them wail, "But she got three jelly beans, and I got two!" demonstrating mathematical skills, critical powers, and a sense of justice all in a single sentence).

Some of this may be a love-struck father's sheer, hopeful projection. But I know that our daughters are growing up imitating, in one way or time or another, Elmo, Mulan, Suzanne Farrell, and Christina Aguilera. That they should inhale and echo a few of their parents' traits and interests, too, should not surprise.

Nancy Verrier cautions that parodies shouldn't be mistaken for the real thing. "Adopted children learn how to please," she says. Parents should be alert to encourage knacks, skills, and qualities inherited from their birth parents, because their children may be reluctant to heed them.

"Adopted children often feel that they have to fit in," she explains. "They're very observant. They're very good at trying to figure how to fit into their families. So we have to be as observant of them as they are of us. I know so many adoptive children who go into professions that they think their parents want them to. There's a lot of people pleasing in adoption. I've worked with some families where you find creative, artistic kids in families full of accountants. But if everyone keeps an open mind, it works."

I'd just add that at this writing, Elise and Lina seem to be on a line to become ballet dancers, avant-garde artists, or Broadway divas. But with all the artists and clowns hanging from limbs on our family tree, I'd be delighted if our daughters showed an inclination to become accountants and tax specialists. I'll be alert for any signs. I'll bring home spreadsheet software, tax forms, and children's biographies of René Descartes if they like. Someone has to take care of the rest of us.

"WHAT ADOPTIVE CHILDREN appreciate most is the parent who understands them," says Nancy Verrier. "They feel closest to those parents who get what's going on with them. If they use their adoption as a starting point, and that wound as a fact of life, rather than a posit, their parents can see them as the person they are."

Nancy remembers a sixteen-year-old girl whom she saw as a patient. She had been adopted at an early age, and seemed equable, if not sunny. She came from a family of accountants. But when she was invited to write poetry, it was filled with anguish and longing that she had rarely shared, and hadn't wanted to. Her parents were good people and fine parents who would have listened, but she didn't want to hurt them.

A Hundred Wounds

"Do PEOPLE who are adopted suffer some kind of primal wound?" Jeffrey Seller asks. "Try a hundred."

Jeff remembers being told that he had been adopted when he was about four, while he rode beside his father in his family's car.

"I think almost every important conversation I can recall having as a kid happened in the car," he says. "People can look just straight ahead. They don't have to look at each other."

Jeff is a man of the theater who recognizes the touches of stagecraft we sometimes rely on in everyday life.

"When I was growing up, I had a strong sense of being an outsider. My partner, Josh, thinks I still have a wound. He says that he can notice the ways in which being adopted still makes me crave approval. But I'm in *show business*," he laughs. "I tell him, 'Everyone around me is like this.' "

Jeff was born in 1964 in suburban Detroit, an unexpected pregnancy for an aging couple who already had three sons and hadn't planned on or prepared for a late-life baby. He was adopted by a family that was going through trying times and was about to have harder times yet. His mother had suffered a series of miscarriages before giving birth to Jeff's older sister. She suffered another before they decided to adopt. Jeff's father had a serious motorcycle accident, health complications, job problems, and depression. He lost the family industrial tool business and became a process server.

"My family was going down the ladder," Jeff remembers of his childhood in Oak Park, Michigan. "Everyone else around us was going up. My parents were not happy or popular people," he says simply. "Our fortunes kept falling. We literally moved to the other side of the tracks."

Jeffrey's father was tall and rugged. His sister was large and struggled with her weight. Jeff always felt conspicuous as "this fair, small little boy."

"You could just look at us and see 'which one of these is not like the other?' But then, I had so many reasons to feel like an outsider. Maybe my wounds have more to do with that."

Jeff was artsy in a family that thought art was a little eccentric. His first stirrings of sexual feeling were, as the expression went then, "different." He was a kid from the other side of the tracks in a community of suburban commuters.

"I had a lot of reasons to feel like an outsider," he says again. "Adoption was just one added to all the others. Was there a wound? Sure. But not just from one knife."

Jeffrey Seller says that he still recalls how his parents, who could not afford an expensive bar mitzvah party, nevertheless threw one for him so that he wouldn't feel slighted among his friends. His sister, who was not adopted, was really the wounded party.

"She felt like I was the favorite child. You know what? She

was right," Jeff says. "My mother had had two miscarriages on her way to having my sister. She did not feel warm toward my sister from the first. My sister felt that and could be a very sad little child." Jeff detects "elfskin" in people: that quality in a performer that makes people want to look at them. "When children are sad," he explains, "adults just don't turn on the lights for them. It's malicious, but it's life. Babies emit something to adults, and adults give it back. I knew I was cherished, so I seemed to be innately friendly. I smiled, and adults smiled back. It made a difference."

Jeffrey's gift for producing smiles proved to be the ticket to his career in the theater. He has produced *Rent,* along with *Avenue Q, In the Heights,* and the 2009 dual-language revival of *West Side Story.* His recollections of his own childhood were sharp enough to make him hesitate when he and Josh began to consider having a family. But if everyone let the pains of childhood discourage them from having children of their own, the history of humankind would have ended with Adam and Eve. Childhood may be as idealized as childbirth.

Jeffrey and Josh have a daughter, May, who is seven, and a six-year-old son named Tommy. Jeff Seller is a sensible, sensitive man who knows that just as art isn't possible without commerce and compromise, you don't grow up without losing things along the way.

"No matter what else is true about adoption," he says, "a birth mother loses something, and her child loses something. We tell our children, 'Some people are good at having children, and some people are good at taking care of them.' " He skips over the example of his own life to say, "We know that our children came to us out of a loss. Their birth mothers lost them. They lost their biological mothers. But they gained two parents who have the love and inclination and psychological means to take care of them and help them grow up. It's loss and gain.

"And you know what?" he continues. "That's life. We lose our teeth. We step out of our diapers. Our hearts get broken. We lose things all the time, and we gain things all the time. The first loss we suffer is one more to add to the pile. There will be more. But there will also be gains. If you never want to get over the first one, I guess you'll never recover. Whether or not it's a wound will depend on the person."

I HAVE A DIM VIEW of parenting guides. Most of them seem just about as comprehensible—and useful—as poorly translated instructions for putting together a toy from Taiwan. However, much of my evaluation is just sheer, pea-brained snobbery, like people who insist that they never watch television yet can sing along with every advertising jingle.

All of the guides about adoption caution parents about the importance of attachment, or the speed and totality with which children who are adopted connect with those who become their parents, the people who are most responsible for nourishing, protecting, and loving them in this world.

Before bed one night, just after I made the rounds to turn

out lights and sprinkle treats into our cat's bowl, I began to thumb through one of those books. It said, as Nancy Verrier suggests, that children who are adopted can be entertainers, eager to superficially please anyone who feeds and cares for them. A child's true state of mind would be visible in his or her drawings.

The authors showed pictures made by children who hadn't "bonded" with their parents. The colors were crayon bright, but the pictures were grim and jarring. Little boys and girls had drawn themselves as small, lonely, fragile stick figures, barely visible in a landscape of sinister clouds and behemoth buildings. No parents were in the pictures, not even staring from a cold, uncaring corner.

I went into my study (that sounds grand—I mean the room in which I write, which also holds the cat litter box), where I tape up pictures that our daughters draw on my shirt cardboards. I snapped on my desk lamp and examined armfuls of their drawings, as if they were treasure maps. There were big yellow smiling suns and twinkling stars, shining down on grinning stick-figure little girls holding hands with their mother and father and each other, and their pets. The people were as big as the buildings. Clouds were soft white pillows. Elise had labeled every figure in every drawing: Mama, Baba(me), Elise, Lina, Leona (our cat), Salman Fishdie (our fish), Cutie Pie and Sweetie Pie (our frogs), and Skeebo, Croakie, and Jo Jo (our hermit crabs). Occasionally our huge stuffed dog, Windy, also appeared.

I snapped off the lamp, latched our apartment door, and slipped into bed beside my wife. I drew my mouth gently against her cheek (never, ever awaken a sleeping mother), and rolled onto my back. My eyes filled. We were a family, and our daughters knew it. They felt it. It was a fact of life as obvious and enduring in their drawings as the sun and the stars.

Of course, they also obviously wanted a dog.

OUR CHILDREN connected with us very quickly. Food, care, and unstinting love had something to do with that; I suppose sheer dependence did, too. Our daughters are affectionate. They play games in which they tire of my constant kissing (Lina went through a period I called Little Lollobrigida, when she would wipe my kiss from her small pink cheek and admonish, "No kissa me!"). But when I theatrically sulk off in despair, they smile, throw their small, soft arms around my neck, and brace themselves for another smooch.

My wife and I are indubitably their mother and father. When they have nightmares or skin their knees, they cry out for Mama. The jump into our bed in the morning and vie to snuggle next to Mama. When something they taste is too hot, spicy, squiggly, or yucky, they don't expel that morsel into a napkin, but Mama's bare hand. When they want a stealthy snack, a made-up story, or a ride on some shoulders, they ask for me.

I tell our daughters stories about a good witch named Beulah, a caramel-corn-eating dolphin named Duncan, and a mermaid named Ethel who bursts into "You'll be swell, you'll be great . . ." at the swish of her tail. The stories are ostensibly recollections from my childhood. But our daughters recommend adjustments to my narratives, like Hollywood producers at a story conference. The final creation wanders in and out of our mingled imaginations and into our dreams. There may be no more enduring bond than that.

But when attachments are strong, there can be sharp anxieties about losing them. Our daughters sometimes seem especially worried about pleasing their mother. Or they seem especially fearful of losing her. Or they get angry with her, as if striking out first is the surest way to avoid being rejected by anyone ever again—a mother especially.

As our girls grow, we have noticed them getting occasional fits of hurt and rage, right on target with all the books that I've disdained. The people at whom they might really be angry, beginning with the rulers who mandate China's one-child policy, are not around to be the targets of their ire. Their parents are right in front of them, arms open. Where better to pour out their bitterest feelings? And what are parents for, if not to try to draw hurts away from our children?

There are times when our daughters have a difficult time with change: saying goodbye, or even goodnight, moving (if even, as we have, across the street), graduating from kindergarten, or ice cream shops that suddenly run out of the sprinkles that they had counted on having. Tantrums are a time-tested way of letting the world, as well as your parents, know that you'd like to call a halt to the rotation of the earth and the momentum of history for one damn minute and make the world *pay attention* to you. This kind of behavior is scarcely unique to children who have been adopted. But some of these ordinary anxieties might pinch a nerve with children who feel that they have been rejected in life before they had a chance to prove how lovable they are.

ONE MORNING Elise padded out early to find me writing and announced that she wanted to make a crown for Lina. The laptop was put aside. We got paper from the printer tray. She carefully drew the spokes of the crown and capped them with stars. I offered to cut the crown from the paper, with all the twists and turns she had drawn in, but Elise insisted on using her small fingers to work the scissors by herself. She snipped, we folded, we taped, and when Lina cried out from her crib, we rushed in to hold the crown over her small, downy head. Then, when we had gauged her proper size and cut the crown to fit, Elise fixed hair clips on two sides to hold it in place. *Princess Paulina!* we proclaimed. Lina beamed as we fussed and smoothed. Her small face burst with utter gladness.

Elise and I hummed an improvised processional as we followed Lina's small strut into the bedroom, where we awakened my wife. *Da-da-da-da! Ladies and Gentlemen, Princess Lina of the Realm of Simon!* We whooped, laughed, and cheered for the best morning ever.

Then Elise decided that she wanted to dress Lina like a

princess, too. She rolled out drawers and dumped boxes, pulling out scarves, jackets, and shirts. She told Lina to stand there while she wrapped and tied. Lina stood still for several minutes, but then she began to bridle at being her sister's dress-up doll. She began to squirm, then stomped away. Elise pinched her, and Lina scampered away, crying and screaming for Mama. I heard a door slam like a cannon shot.

By the time I got to her room, Elise was ripping the exquisite crown she had made for her sister into twenty and thirty little tiny angry pieces. Her face had hardened like a fist. Her bright brown eyes smoldered with tears. I slid down to the floor with my back against the wall.

"First, don't pinch," I said. "If you're angry, use words." But Elise had been told that scores of times before. Just repeating that commandment now was as useful as pouring water over a stone. She felt pinched—punched, really—by what she took to be Lina's rejection. After all the drawing, coloring, ornate cutting, fiddling, draping, dressing, and getting things just so, her little sister had pushed her away and scurried off to claim their mother's arms. Elise felt rejected; then replaced. We tell our daughters, "Use your words, darling." But what words would a six-year-old—or a sixty-year-old—know for whatever feelings were cooking and competing in Elise then?

"Don't pinch. Ever," I said more softly. Then, after I had said what duty required, I uttered what I knew I had really walked into the room to tell her, even as the words leaped out of my heart ahead of me: "I love you. Your mother loves you. Your sister loves you. Leona loves you. Sammi loves you. Your aunts, uncles, and grandparents, your teachers and the people who work downstairs at the market and the cleaners and the drugstore and the pizza place and the Chinese restaurant all love you. I don't know much about nuclear energy or rocket science. But I am sure—absolutely, positively, a thousand percent sure—that the strongest force on earth is the love I have for you."

Elise cocked an eye.

"Where's da crown?" she asked. I had picked up the pieces and put them on a shelf behind me. "Here, baby," I said, turning them over to her.

Elise tucked the scraps against her chest and walked away. I followed her footsteps through the hall, into a foyer, into the dining room, and finally into the kitchen where, I was sure, she would present the sad, torn pieces of the lacerated crown to Lina and say "I'm sorry." We would tape them together and have breakfast on the balcony. Bluebirds would sit on our shoulders, chirping cheerfully and passing jars of honey on their wings.

Lina was clasping her mother's knees when we got to the kitchen. Elise reared back with her fistful of paper pieces and heaved them at their feet.

"Stupid poo-poo head!" she shrieked. "I hate you, stupid Mama stupid Baba stupid stupid stupid Lina poo-poo heads!"

Well, she used her words . . .

Caroline held Elise while I picked up Lina. Elise pulled back, she sputtered into my wife's face, and she screamed. No words: just screamed. She spat, she shrieked, she fumed. She pulled out of Caroline's embrace, like Ali slipping out of a headlock against the ropes, and reached up to hit Lina's foot. She was aiming for her back. When I turned away from that attempted assault, she changed strategy and thwacked my rump. *Stupid Lina stupid stupid Baba poo-poo head.* It is hard to watch a child you love spew hurt, spittle, and wrath. After a couple of rounds with no decision, she went back to my wife's arms, and this time she stayed and cried. And cried some more.

But within ten minutes (which was probably more like twenty), she was at the kitchen table eating matzo and hummus (no doubt this paragraph makes it all seem so much easier than it really was). Demons had overtaken our daughter. But she was learning to beat them back, and that took grit and character. Our apartment was still standing, and our younger daughter was still whole. I admired Elise. She had earned her matzo and hummus—breakfast of champions.

CHILDREN HAVE TANTRUMS whether they've been adopted from China, plucked from bulrushes, or born into the House of Windsor. I don't believe that children who have been adopted have any more or fewer tantrums than did Lhamo Döndrub (and he grew up to be the fourteenth Dalai Lama).

But those children who have been adopted from China, Russia, Ethiopia, or institutions here have had lives that we weren't there to share. For our daughters, that meant spending months in orphanages in which they may have been well fed but not always well attended to.

To our daughters, and perhaps other children who have spent their first, formative months in institutions, hunger (or cold, or feeling left alone) may not be just a pang in the stomach but what professionals call a trigger. That twinge doesn't tell them: *You're hungry. What'll it be? I see your folks have got bananas, yogurt, bagels, milk, soymilk, carrots, crackers, leftover pizza, guacamole, biriyani, and four different kinds of cereals spilling out of the pantry and refrigerator shelves. Enjoy!* Instead, pangs can set off old feelings, if not memories, of howling for food and waiting, reaching up to be held and having no one pick you up and hold you close. A flash of hunger can make children who've spent their first months in institutions feel threatened and vulnerable. It can make them cling and claw, and can light a fuse to the fright, fight, or flight reflex.

My wife and I have learned to think about our children the way a baseball manager thinks of his pitchers: You have to know when to pull them. They may look good and seem strong after a hundred pitches. But you have to take them out of the game before the first twinge of fatigue can make them do something you'll both regret. Take them away, get them food and rest. Don't wait until you see them begin to wind down.

And don't be reluctant—or too prideful about the profound attachment that you enjoy with your children—to bring in help. Let them get on the ground and play with and talk to professionals who have seen five hundred other children act like this, children from China, Russia, or Scarsdale. Do it while children are just pinching and shouting "Stupid poo-poo head!" Do it to spare them unnecessary months or even years of angry fits and moods that can't be much fun for them, either.

Our daughters are our babies; they always will be. But if they wanted for food, warmth, or attention in their first, formative months, they lost a few months of pure, innocent infancy before we ever got to them. They couldn't assume love in those first few weeks and months when they had just left their mother's body, and they must have felt suddenly and unnaturally responsible for their own survival.

I think that the love my wife and I give our daughters can help bind whatever wound they have and make them strong. It may even, after a time, help make the wound almost undetectable. Indeed, our daughters' sense of being responsible for themselves will be an adult asset. But first, they need and deserve a chance to be children.

My wife and I often feel that our lives did not truly begin until we met our children (actually, I say that *my* life didn't begin until I met Caroline; friends who have known me all my life agree). But it's only wise for us to remember that our daughters' lives did not begin with us. Come to think of it, remembering that someone else's life did not begin the moment we met them is something good for most of us to recall in any relationship, whether with friends, spouses, or foreign countries.

Cold, Mama, Cold

WHEN ELISE was about two, Caroline and I put her into bed between us on a winter's night in Chicago. At some point, she stirred and shivered. The sheet and blankets had slipped off her as she squirmed, and she called out to Caroline—or perhaps to the world?—"Cowd, Mama, cowd!"

Caroline hiked the blankets back up around her chin. We both hugged her. Our baby, huddled and shivering, calling out for her mother's touch. Trusting that all she had to do was call, and her mother would be there.

Elise had no memory of that moment the next day. But since then, she's heard the story plenty. It's become a comedy routine between us. When we cross a windy Michigan Avenue or Broadway corner, she shouts, "Cowd, Baba, cowd!" to me, even though she now pronounces her l's as precisely as a member of the Royal Shakespeare Company. "*Cowd*, Baba, *cowd*!"

But one night a few years later as Caroline tucked her into bed, Elise asked about how her mother had left her in front of the factory in China. She was wrapped in a blanket, Caroline told her. All clean, the tiny little blanket pulled up to her chin.

"Was I cold?" Elise asked.

Caroline took a breath.

"No, darling. Your mother loved you. She watched to make certain that you were found and were all right. She made sure you had clothing and a blanket. You were *not* cold."

A while later, all of the circumstances we usually try to avoid conspired. We were in a restaurant with some family members, and service was slow. Dinner dragged on. Children scampered. Crayons wore down. It edged past nine. Our girls erupted. Caroline took them outside, with apologies. I scooped up Elise's shoes, Caroline's purse, and two of Lina's stuffed animals and joined them on the sidewalk. People stared and shook their heads. I glimpsed a few smiles of the kind that usually say "Boy, do I remember" (or "Glad it's not me"). I hailed a cab. It was one of those moments when you wonder, "Will anyone ask, 'What are those two white people doing packing two screaming young Asian girls into a taxicab?' " But this is America. The driver (an Iranian man) said, "Hey, my son cries like that."

Elise held on tight. She began to yawn as she sobbed into Caroline's shoulder.

"I didn't get enough to eat," Elise said.

"You left plenty of food on your plate back there," Caroline pointed out. "If you were hungry, you should have eaten it."

"No. *In her stomach,*" said Elise, "I was always hungry. *Why weren't you there?*"

My darlings, we came as soon as we could.

Like Steve Levitt, I do not think it is possible that our daughters possess any actual memories of their first months. But as we tell them the little that we know of their stories, their imaginations improvise the missing parts that we cannot know. As they get older and smarter, they will realize how little we really know, and anxieties may take their place; they often do.

(Elise told us the next day that when she was in her birth mother's stomach, she was fed only broccoli—any child's nightmare.)

So while I don't accept the idea that children who are adopted suffer a primal wound, I believe that they may have to deal with some kind of fundamental anxiety about how they came to their place in the world. And as my wife recounted for me the words of comfort that she cooed (in French) into our daughter's sleepy, weepy face, I found myself wondering how many of us would have been reassured to hear such a speech on some of our worst days of growing up:

"When you're young, you want to be like everyone else," she told Elise. "I know. People used to make fun of my hair, my clothes, my accent. But when you're older, you'll see that it's good to be different. You don't want to be like everybody else. The things that make you different make you more interesting. We went all the way around the world to get you. When you're older—just a little older—you'll realize that everything you think is a problem now is actually something good. They'll be your strong points. And you will be strong."

"I Was Never in Her Shoes"

EVERY ADOPTION STORY has both its own place and time. For our daughters, it begins with being born in China under laws that oppress millions. But our girls also belong to a distinct group of 55,000 or so babies from China who have been adopted by families in the West. Studies, books, and movies will purport to follow their progress as a group, what Anchee Min has called "the little blossoms from China."

Steve Sagri was part of a less publicized program. Not so long ago, some Western nations also shipped away children who had been cast aside.

Steve was born in the port city of Ancona, Italy, in 1952. His mother was the kind of woman who is often enviously described as a free spirit—a poet, writer, operagoer, a passionate woman who did not always contemplate or accept responsibility for passion's consequences. Steve has discovered that she had some Jewish lineage, which, with complicit friends, she took care to obscure in Fascist Italy, changing her name from Segré to Sagri. He says that it was known around town that his mother wrote some Fascist propaganda for people in power and had other opportunistic liaisons with local army commanders and officials.

"I don't criticize," Steve declares. "She had to survive. I was never in her shoes."

Steve does not know his father. "I just have my suspicions," he says with a small, spiritless laugh. His mother placed him in the local orphanage shortly after his birth. She had a small apartment and it was hard to provide for children in the deprivation, rubble, and disorder of postwar Italy.

"A *Catholic* orphanage," Steve stresses, although there was no other kind in Ancona at the time. "That way, if anything happened again, we'd be protected." It was one thing that a mother as harmed by history as Steve's could do for her son: put him someplace that Jewish children might be safe should Fascists return.

"At least that's what I like to think," he adds.

Steve spent most of his first years in two different orphanages, seeing his mother only on weekends or an occasional weekday. She had another son, with another father, and Steve acquired a brother, Alphonse, who got sent to the same orphanage. Their mother died when Steve was nine and his brother just over a year old, apparently of a heart condition.

Steve says he was not surprised. He had never seen her free spirit very happy.

Catholic Charities had a program then that permitted American families to take in children from Italian orphanages. Two years later, in August 1963, Steve and his brother landed in New York. He remembers their first meal, eaten in a dank, sweltering welfare hotel: baloney (in no way to be confused with Bologna) sandwiches on Wonder Bread. Steve looked around at slimy walls crawling with insects, heard wailing sirens in the night, and looked down at a meager meal between two spongy tissue slices.

"This is America?" he says he asked. "Where are the streets paved with gold?"

Steve and his brother were adopted by an Italian American family that lived in Hillside, Illinois. They had a son who was younger than Steve and older than Al. "Things just didn't work out," Steve says, with more graciousness than seems necessary. The couple conspicuously favored the son who had been born to them. When Al wet his bed, he was beaten for it. To this day, Steve says that he cannot fathom why the couple ever thought that they wanted to bring two more children into their home. They seemed only cold and suspicious toward the boys. Steve wonders today if the family was trying only to impress their priest or qualify for some kind of stipend.

One day, the brothers were taken for a car ride and saw a

skyline looming. "Are we going to Chicago?" Steve asked.
They were—to the Angel Guardian Orphanage on the north
side.

"They sat my brother on the counter," Steve recalls. "Just
left us there, like some kind of delivery parcel."

Steve and his brother stayed at Angel Guardian for about
a year and a half, until Steve made it through the eighth
grade. Then they were moved to Hoosier Boys Town, a community for orphans and youngsters from troubled families
that had been founded by the venerable Father Michael Cam-
pagna. Boys Town was located on lovely, rolling grounds in
an Indiana suburb of Chicago. It was run by compassionate
Chicago priests and exacting Italian nuns, and it received generous support from prominent Chicago mobsters who were
keen to be regarded by their church, if not by the Illinois
Crime Commission, as civic benefactors.

"Those holiday parties!" Steve still remembers. "The food,
the desserts, the gifts . . ."

A family who wanted a younger child eventually adopted
Al. Steve became the only boy in Boys Town who didn't have
at least one older relative—an uncle, a distant cousin—who
came to visit. An older couple named Stoney and Dolly Monestere came to Boys Town and asked Father Michael if they
could take a boy home for the Christmas holidays. Steve went
home with them and eventually spent weekends and other
holidays in their home. Modern readers may be tempted to
reproach the couple for not taking Steve into their family full

time. But they were older, not set up for children, and besides, in the 1960s, Hoosier Boys Town was considered almost a prep school among orphanages. Short of being adopted by a Kennedy, Boys Town was considered just about the most advantageous background you could give a child who had lost his parents.

Steve says that in later years he heard that Stoney Monestere told his friends that he had come to consider Steve a son to him. But he never said that to Steve. Steve, meanwhile, says, "I never had a father, so I made one up." He began to fantasize that his father must have been a valiant Royal Air Force pilot who had helped liberate Italy in 1944 (the math doesn't quite work out for a son born eight years later, but of course, it's a fantasy). He told himself that one of Britain's noblest few didn't know that he'd fathered a son with the wild, free-spirited woman with whom he had spent a weekend to dispel the loneliness and grimness of war. Steve told himself that if only he knew, he would surely come soaring back.

But he had no interest in reaching the man that he had good reason to believe was his father. Steve was certain that in reality he would only be rejected—again.

TODAY STEVE LIVES in suburban Cleveland and is one of the most successful vendors and scholars of fine timepieces in the United States. He also flies, paints, dives, takes award-winning photographs (including a joyful, poignant portrait of small boys in an Italian orphanage), and studies martial arts.

Steve Sagri seems to do nothing casually. When he takes a photograph, it's to win first place. When he dives, it's to find treasure. He is among the busiest, most effective people I know. He says that the circumstances of how he was born and how he grew up have everything to do with becoming the accomplished and interesting man that he is today—and that's the problem.

"I haven't had an exactly successful family life," he volunteers. He was close to his brother, Al, but has had three marriages, producing two children.

"But even with my daughters, even when they were adorable little kids, I never felt real comfortable," he says. "I never knew how to behave around them. I didn't know how to be a parent. How would I? I'd never seen it done. I still feel awkward when I talk to them. And it really hurts because I know it's my fault. It comes from me, and something I've never been able to come to terms with. Maybe I should have gone into therapy thirty years ago, except people didn't do that then. I see other people and know that I've missed out on a hell of a lot." This from a man who goes from oceans to skies.

"We have a forty-five-hundred-square-foot house," Steve notes, "and I can't stay at home for more than five minutes. I always have to keep *moving*. I can't settle into anything. If we go antiquing, I can't just look, I have to take pictures. I study martial arts even though, at this point, how much more can I learn? It's the constant fear, I guess. That something will happen. That I always have to be *ready*. That I always might have to *move*.

"Maybe my real fear is of getting hurt," he muses. "Maybe that's why I've built so many ten-foot walls around me. Maybe it's because I was rejected as a kid that I don't want to give anyone the chance to reject me now. So I just keep moving. If you always expect rejection, you'll never be disappointed, right? Or so I tell myself. Or so I think.

"No doubt about it. I blame myself. And I blame my mother for a lot. She gave me up. She didn't care. Then she took the easy way out by dying, so she'd never have to see me or my brother again."

"Well, you can't really tell . . ." I begin to gently suggest to Steve, but he preempts me.

"I may not like her, but I don't criticize," he repeats. "I wasn't in her shoes."

THIS IS WHERE a friend needs to step in. I will, because I know Steve as a generous and thoughtful friend, and I don't believe that that quality comes from nothing. He says he may be more comfortable with friends because he can pull back with them and not hurt or disappoint as he would with a spouse or child. "I get close, I get fearful," he says. "That's the story of my life."

Steve says that he wouldn't mind getting a call or a note some day from a Segré who claimed to be related. "But I'd have to wonder," he says. "What do they want from me? Is that the only reason they called? I guess I'm not set up for emotional joy."

I think that at this point in his life, Steve has earned some of the same generosity of spirit he would extend in judgment of a friend. We know one of Steve's daughters. She's a fine young woman, just beginning a career in law. She has known Steve's warmth and love, even if he wishes he had been better at it. Those of us who know his capacity for kindness can wish that Steve Sagri and his brother, born to a restless, charming woman who spurned the chance to be a mother to her children, had found the love of an adoptive family.

Love Above and Beyond

STEPHEN SEGALLER figures that he's always had the ability to discover more about his birth parents, but hasn't seized an opportunity. Stephen was born in postwar England and adopted on what he calls a "prehistoric private basis." His mother and father, Joyce and Denis, felt it would be a good idea for their ten-year-old son to have a brother. So a family friend arranged for them to meet a young woman who was about to have a baby.

The young woman had an Irish name. About ten years ago, Stephen learned that his birth mother was an Irish nurse who had immigrated to Great Britain. He has inferred that his birth father was probably a doctor, with the Irish nurse's pregnancy handled as a hushed-up embarrassment in a village hospital. That story seems more plausible than Steve Sagri's valiant RAF fighter pilot father fantasy, but Stephen has so far chosen not to undertake any of the kind of investigation that might resolve all doubt. His mother, Joyce, lives in a nursing home now, and he sweeps aside all the bromidic notions that he worries his mother would feel rejected or betrayed by any discoveries.

"It would just seem like second-guessing," says Stephen, "of .one of the great things you can do for a human being, which is to adopt them and love them."

Stephen says that his mother told him his birth mother made just one request: that the child to whom she was about to give birth be raised as a Catholic.

"Oh, don't worry," he says his mother told her. "We're atheists. We won't raise him with any religion at all."

Stephen was never close to the brother for whom he was supposed to be some kind of balancing presence. They were ten and a half years apart in age—almost the same signature difference as Elvis Presley and the Beatles—and didn't play football in the park, bicycle, listen to the Troggs, or dance the frug together. "More of an affectionate uncle," Stephen explains. They're closer now for what they've shared as adults.

Stephen has learned that his birth mother already had a little girl, which would have complicated her plight even more and made her decision to find a family—quickly—for the baby that she was about to have even clearer.

"To have a half or full sibling somewhere—that is a kind of resonant or a provocative thought," says Stephen. But so far, only a thought.

"What I know is enough to know for the moment," he says. "And I suppose the prospect of some awkward surprise is always in the back of my mind. What if I meet some people to whom I am related, and I discover that we have nothing truly important in common and I just don't want to be part of their lives?"

Stephen's father was an accomplished linguist, and Stephen evinced a gift for languages—Latin, Greek, French, German, Spanish, Italian—at an early age. His school gave him a battery of tests. He apparently scored well. The headmaster said, "I'd like to know more about that boy's father," figuring any discoveries could contribute a case study to the ongoing argument about how to gauge the relative importance of nature and nurture in personality and aptitudes. Could Stephen's talents all be attributed to the father who had adopted him? Or was there also a trace to be discovered in the history of his birth father? The more we discover about DNA, the more impressive its influence.

"But the more we learn about genetics," Stephen points out, "the more it seems to be a lottery anyway." He has produced, among many other television programs in the United States and Great Britain, the series *A Question of Genes: Inherited Risks*. There is no genetic guarantee that Stephen Hawking's children can balance a checkbook any better than descendants of the engineers who forgot to make the metric conversions for the $125 million Mars orbiter that they mistakenly sent sailing past the planet in 1999.

"I have to answer NA—not applicable—on a lot of medical stuff," says Stephen Segaller. "I have no information on any hereditary illnesses. I don't know anything about any history of cancer or diabetes, and I'm not sure my life would be more intelligible or richer if I did know." (Whereas our daughters have been relieved—no, giddy and delighted—to learn that because we have no genetic link, they cannot inherit diabetes from me.)

Stephen grew up devoutly unchurched. When he came home from school and said something favorable about so much as the music of any religious observance that the school had required him to attend, his parents would grumble, "Rubbish, absolute rubbish."

When Stephen was thirteen, some sporting exploit got him written up—"for the first and last time, I assure you"—in the local *Surrey Advertiser.* His parents got a phone call. A woman introduced herself as the young athlete's cousin. Stephen said she came out for "a very genteel tea," during which she reported to Stephen's father that they belonged to an extended Jewish family. In a way, it seemed more startling—and certainly more pertinent and revealing—for Stephen to hear this than anything that he might learn about his birth parents.

Joyce and Denis's marriage fell apart. Ironically, his

mother then spent some of her happiest years teaching physical education in a Catholic school in which the nuns cherished her and she revered the nuns, their devotion to organized spiritual rubbish notwithstanding. Stephen's father went to work for UNESCO, where the atheist who had never suspected that he was in any trace Jewish became a Buddhist. Stephen's mother pronounced that as perfect, for reasons that an ex-wife is entitled to observe and that Stephen dismisses with bemusement.

He says that he knew strongly, from the age of fourteen or fifteen, that he wanted to be a parent, not just a father. He loved babies. He loved being around children. Stephen got married, and when he and his wife, Merrill, had a son and a daughter, he says that she joshed that he wanted to breast-feed them. He even looked forward to three A.M. feedings as a chance to hold his children close and hear their gurgles against his ear.

STEPHEN SEGALLER is head of national production for a great metropolitan television station (WNET, New York), and he is known as (to rely on a single word) a gentleman. He shows up on time. He keeps his word. He returns calls and treats people with respect—all traits so rare in broadcasting they are practically regarded as Gandhian.

He says that he cannot recall ascribing any of the usual insecurities of childhood or adolescence to being adopted.

"I am tempted to say it's the opposite," he ventures.

"When you are the person who is the object of a voluntary act of love and commitment, it's a tremendously affirming experience. I mean, what greater sense of value can you give to a baby or a child than to say, 'We are going to embrace you, and commit to give our lives to you'?

"Pregnancies can be accidental," he reminds us. "Adoptions never are. Those of us who are adopted have every reason to feel snug and secure. Loved above and beyond, really."

DENIS HAS DIED, and Joyce Segaller is fading a bit now, living in a nursing home in Great Britain. Stephen says that when he comes to visit, the every-second-of-every-day exasperations and indignities of walking, sitting, eating, seeing, hearing, and going to the bathroom seem to have pushed his mother's emotions closer to the surface. Stephen brought along his son, the actor Adam Segaller, on a recent visit. Adam hadn't seen his grandmother for a couple of years. Realistically, when might he ever see her again?

Stephen Segaller says that he and his son took turns to bend down and kiss his mother in her chair. Before Adam could step back she grabbed his arm and gripped his hand in her own.

"You know, Adam," she told him, "that's the best thing I've ever done in my life. Standing right behind you."

There is a long pause and an audible rasp of his office chair before Stephen asks, "How much more of a parent do I need to go and find than that?"

Don't Be Afraid to Ask

"CAN I LOVE someone else's child as much as I would love my own?"

I've been asked that question by dozens of people, who invariably seem apologetic and embarrassed. My own answer is short and explicit ("Yes! Yes! At least as much and more!"). But I try to answer with respect for the candor, even the nerve, that it takes to pose the question to someone who, from all the evidence, could be offended.

Any parent must wonder whether they can love *any* child. They're endearing, yes. But children howl, mewl, and throw up on your best clothes. They interrupt your happy life. It is not villainous to ask ourselves if we really want to admit these demanding interlopers into our future. When a baby is the result of nature's taking its course, you can hardly argue that it's not meant to be. But why go out of your way?

My wife and I knew that Elise and Lina were our babies from the moment we received their postage-stamp portraits. Logically, I know that's not possible. But I also know that's how my heart, mind, and body—my very chromosomes, I am quite sure—reacted to their pictures. This little girl was on the other side of the world. But somehow, she needed *us*. I felt a real, physical ache to hold her. Every day, if I had wanted, I could have set aside time to worry about the millions of children left to languish in the orphanages of China. But I didn't.

Then one day, one of those multitudes was made a part of our family. It was just on forms and in a picture, but I suddenly felt the tugging of some huge extraordinary cord from the other side of the globe, and I knew that no power on earth would keep us away from that child. We would kick down the Great Wall of China to get to her.

I would take the photo out of my wallet in the weeks before we left to get each of our girls and hold it against my lips to whisper, "We're coming, baby." Something inside was set off by seeing those faces and knowing they had been set in the path of my life. I heard a call. I don't know what kinds of wiring genes and nature have provided. But think that's how human beings have been conditioned for centuries: to take care of children who have been cast aside. No matter how or from whom they began, they become ours.

AFTER ALL THE BOOKS and workshops that warned about hard stares and careless remarks, we've had a far bigger problem almost missing planes because people coo, ooh, and try to amuse our daughters.

"Are the two of you sisters?" many ask. Elise steps up.

"Yes. We're from the same province," she adds, sometimes shaking a finger. "But not the same orphanage."

I suppose that some people are moved to stop us because we are not, after all, complete strangers to them (they've heard or seen me; they've heard about us). Many people seem touched by the beauty of our family (with me, the toad, holding up the back end) and what they infer from it. Sometimes we want to tell them, "Adorable? Yes. But you ought to try getting them to put their shoes on. You ought to try telling them that they can't have another jelly vitamin. You ought to try . . ."

We don't want our girls to be walking advertisements for anything (unless it's Chanel or Hermès and contracts have been signed). We want them to be free to have tantrums and spew at their parents without feeling that they somehow disappoint people by being human.

But even at that, a few tantrums ago, Elise wound up crying and pounding the floor in an airport after a long day (what traveler hasn't wanted to do that?). I sat on the floor to be with her while she cried the demons out. Then she began to scream them out. My wife stood a few steps away holding Lina, who squirmed in her arms to join Elise's fun on the floor. People walked by, smiling. It occurred to me later: What made everyone so sure that the squalling, crying, raging little girl pounding her fists into the ground was ours?

I guess it was the way that the four of us took each other for granted, the way we do in families: something that says, even in a shrug or rolling eye, that we'll wait this out together.

Kind of an Average Guy

CHRIS LEONARD is one of those people who make it a point to call themselves "kind of an average guy." Are they ever?

Chris is forty-one and lives in North Carolina, where he works in a corner office for a furniture manufacturer, developing marketing systems and support functions. In his younger, wilder days he "did something in computers" in graphics and printing. He grew up in Lexington, North Carolina, went to Appalachian State, and always knew that his parents, Briggs and Glenda Leonard, had adopted him through the Children's Home Society.

"I don't remember a time that I didn't know. I don't remember anyone telling me for the first time. My parents were always willing to talk about it. They never made me feel that it was something that shouldn't be talked about. It was there, like my hair color. But no big thing."

Chris, in fact, has sandy-red hair, now graying gently, and figures that might have drawn more attention to him as he grew up than the fact that he had been adopted.

"You know kids," he says. "I can remember one or two times when someone tried to dig at me. But it never really worked. Being adopted was no big thing to much of anybody. My parents just always made me feel loved and lucky—even if I didn't know then how truly damn lucky I was."

Chris met his wife, Karen, while they were both in college,

and discovered that they had both been adopted. They considered themselves blessed and fortunate, but they didn't talk about sharing that circumstance so much as knowing that they did made them (or at least Chris) feel that it could go unspoken. "Maybe it's a male-female thing," he laughs. "Guys seem not to want to talk about any of that stuff. Women seem to feel that you have to talk about everything."

Karen spoke about finding her birth mother and father one day. Chris told her that he was just never interested, or at least interested enough to take any steps to discover who had brought him into being.

"I never idealized or fantasized about birth parents," he said. "They just had no place in my thoughts whatever. I thought, 'Yes, there may be people out there, maybe not, and good people, or maybe not. But if it ain't broke, don't fix it.' I guess that's what I thought."

Chris was in Philadelphia on business and Karen had flown up to join him for a Van Morrison concert. They came back home to find a FedEx slip under the door, and the next morning, a uniformed employee delivered a letter to Chris Leonard from his birth mother.

Her name was Diane. At age seventeen she had had a brief "relationship" (a real genteelism) with a charming local bad boy, who she sensed was not the great love of her life. But she wanted to have her baby. She and her sister shared a single room in Durham, and she was not prepared to be a parent. But she wanted to have her baby.

"It was—it is—the most beautiful letter in the world," Chris Leonard says. "I will cherish it till the day I die. The real gist of it was: I was wanted. I may not have been planned, and I may not have been kept. But I was definitely wanted.

"She saw me three times in the month after she had me, while they found a family. Now, as a father myself"—two boys and a girl—"I realize what a hard thing she went through to do the best thing for me. She didn't have me 'taken care of.' Even if she couldn't care for me, as a mother. She had me, and loved me, and did the best thing that she could do for me."

Chris and Karen remembered what it had been like to hold their first child, Justin, in their arms, look down into his face, and see evidence of their own faces. To grasp their baby's delicate toy fingers, and feel their hearts racing. Someone else, created from you, was alive and needy. They could not imagine how a seventeen-year-old girl had found the courage and love to do what Diane did: bring her child into the world, then put him in a better position to be happy.

Chris told his parents, Briggs and Glenda, that they needed to get together. Family business. Briggs and Glenda thought that Chris and Karen must be expecting again. Well, yes, in a way. Chris showed them Diane's letter. He pointed to a line in which she said, "If I never hear from you, I understand."

"And I understand," Chris told his parents, "if you don't want me to write back or ever see her. After what you did for me . . ." He explains now, "They, not Diane, were absolutely my primary concern. I knew they would support me, even if it hurt them. But I didn't want to hurt them. I had to be sure they weren't just covering up. Once again, as parents do, not letting on that we've hurt them. Hell, I didn't know what I thought."

Briggs and Glenda Leonard said that Diane sounded like a fine woman who had made a mistake, handled it well, and now deserved to meet the son she had done so much for.

They met at a nice restaurant in Raleigh. Diane came with her two children. They had known about Chris all their lives, and even observed his birthday (September 23). The four of them just stood there, teary-eyed and grinning.

"This almost-sixty-year-old woman," says Chris, "standing there with all of us, and I looked more like her than her kids did, and everyone in the room could see it. I wonder what the hell they must have thought."

DIANE ASKED CHRIS at some point, "Would you like to see a picture of your birth father?"

Diane had a picture. You wouldn't need to be a master spy to detect a flabbergasting resemblance. Chris Leonard and the man in the photo had the same graceful profile, the same slight slope to the forehead. They had the same grayish sandy-red hair, albeit in different proportions. Now that Chris was pushing forty, he could also see their hairlines receding along the same contours. The man in the photo had an assertive grin. He knew how to hold himself and smile into a lens, and not just at birthday parties and sales department awards luncheons.

Chris, who had once been a graphic artist, could tell that the photo had been carefully and artfully composed. The face wasn't familiar (except that it was similar to the one Chris saw in his mirror), but it radiated celebrity. The man wore conspicuously fine clothes, carefully tailored. He had a beard, so Chris thought that he must be some Hollywood figure, a producer, director, or celebrity agent.

Chris looked at the photo and said to himself, "That's the prick that didn't care about anything other than himself."

"It's Alexander Julian," Diane told him.

The name was faintly familiar, but no more than any other you could glance past in the boldface of celebrity columns that Chris glossed over. Chris Leonard had to Google his birth father. Alexander Julian had won five Coty Awards and been on the International Best Dressed List nine times. But the first item that made any kind of connection with Chris was the one that read "Redesigned the University of North Carolina Tarheels men's basketball uniforms."

"Then I knew I'd heard of him," said Chris.

(A short personal detour here. Alex Julian is a very close friend, whom my family and I love very much. In fact, we are extended family: Caroline and Alex's wife, Meagan, are cousins; our daughters consider their sons and daughters their cousins. Caroline and I were married at Alex's house. He is one of the best, kindest, most generous human beings, a devoted husband and father, and an artful designer; if you're wearing brightly colored men's underwear, you have Alex to thank. He and Meagan have a warm, close, wonderful marriage and family that they have built over more than twenty years. But there was a time in his life when Alex would have been voted Father of the Year only if the title were awarded on the basis of sheer volume. As he said to me once, "I was one of the few straight designers on the street, and I didn't let that go to waste.")

Chris read on, and nothing that he read moved him to try to reach his birth father. Diane seemed to be just a small-town secret stashed in Alex's glitzy, jet-setting life, and Chris felt suddenly and urgently loyal to the woman who had delivered and given him up, with great grief and heartbreak, while this satyr galloped off to New York and Rome. Chris Leonard is a loving and responsible father. He looked at Alex Julian's picture and thought, "We have nothing in common except that we look alike." And while he didn't like Alex at a distance, he didn't want to risk hurting a stranger by unveiling a new son in his life.

"I'm a guy. I was a young guy," says Chris. "I can't say that I wouldn't have done the same thing."

And he didn't want Diane to be hurt again by any of the human clutter that can fall out of a family attic when you go digging for skeletons. "It was pretty clear to me," says Chris, "that Alex was a lot more important to her than she had ever been to him."

A YEAR and a half passed. Chris's anger cooled. As he notes now, Alex and Diane have different recollections of the period in which Chris was conceived and born. Chris wants to be a son, not a detective or judge.

Chris went to a furniture show in Las Vegas for his firm. As he and some coworkers and friends ranged around hotels for meetings and receptions, he saw placards showing a man with a grayish sandy-red beard, grinning over his new furniture line.

And then Chris Leonard saw his birth father on the casino floor of the MGM Grand. Bells pealed, lights sizzled, and silver dollars clanged—but then, it was Las Vegas. Alex and Meagan were strolling through the gaming floor, not twenty feet from Chris. He almost ripped an arm off a friend who was standing with him. "You know who that is?" he asked. His friend knew the story.

Chris decided to follow Alex and Meagan, but then couldn't find them. He went to a company cocktail party, but couldn't carry on a coherent conversation. He stalked out, dazed and sweating, and walked the casino floor for an hour and a half. He must have seen ten thousand people, but not Alexander Julian. He had a drink—alone. He went to bed. He stared up at the ceiling and out his window at the skyscape of rippling neon lights and thought: "It's different seeing him in person. Seeing the picture, he's Alexander Julian. Famous guy I don't know. Some guy who wasn't there. Seeing him in person, I felt something. He was there now. I felt something."

Alex left Las Vegas the next morning. But like a lot of famous people, he is almost ridiculously easy to contact. Chris
called Alex's studio in Connecticut, and the next thing he
knew . . .

He pauses in telling the story. "I don't want any of this to
hurt him," he says. "I don't want any of this to hurt him or
reflect badly on him in any way. I love him. I can't hurt him.
How many guys do exactly what he did and walk away and
we never know? He's not the same man that he was forty
years ago.

"I thought it was better to call him than it even would
have been to go up to him on the floor," says Chris. "I didn't
know if Meg knew." She didn't; but she knew the man she
had married. "I said . . . I don't remember. Something like,
'You knew a girl named Diane. Well, she's my mother, and
you're my father. I don't want anything from you. I just happened to be in Las Vegas and saw you. I'm married and have
three kids and I'm doing just fine. I don't need anything. I'd
just like to meet you sometime. How would you feel about
that?' And Alex said, 'I got tears streaming down my face.
Does that tell you anything?' "

Chris says that Alex told him he needed a few moments to
absorb the new fact of a birth son that he'd never met, and
three grandchildren he hadn't known he had. Chris offered to
email a picture of himself to Alex. He had seen exquisite photographs of Alex's family on various websites and told him,
"I think you'll see something."

Chris sent off the picture of himself: sandy-red beard, grayish sandy-red hair. Alex phoned two minutes later.

"Well," he said, "I guess we don't need a paternity test."

"I AM ONE LUCKY, in fact *the* luckiest son of a bitch in the world," says Chris Leonard. He and Karen and their children met Alex, Meagan, and their children. Civility quickly melted into real warmth. The Leonards are genuine, interesting people who have their own busy lives in North Carolina, but they come to Connecticut every few months. Alex and Meg, who maintain family and business links in North Carolina, are there for long weekends, outings, and the birthday parties and grade school graduations of Chris and Karen's three children: Alex and Meg's grandchildren. The Julians have a large, loving, and complicated family that cannot be described with the usual designations, lineage trees, flow, and genealogy. Meg's graciousness and Alex's kindness are the source of warmth at the center of it.

"Things couldn't have gone better," says Chris, which is what Karen, Alex, Meg, Diane, and everyone else says, too.

In fact, the situation has turned out so happily that Alex and Meagan felt that they had to caution their teenage sons. They were delighted that Chris, Karen, and their children had become a part of their lives. But they have told their boys not to imitate their father's approach for starting families.

"I'm sure there are things he doesn't like about who he used to be," Chris says of Alex (and he is "Alex" when Chris speaks of him to me, and not "my father"). "What he was doesn't matter to me. I have two great, wonderful parents. And now, a great relationship with two other birth parents. My life would have been great, just great, if I'd never found out and none of it had happened. But now that it has, how much richer is my life to know two more people who love and look out for me?"

HE IS GLAD that he was almost forty, and a husband and father, by the time Diane decided to find him. "I was stable and secure and could deal with it," Chris says. "Versus me when I was eighteen, twenty, or twenty-five."

Chris was not only stable and secure, but reacted with instinctive kindness when he read a letter from a woman who had put the deepest hope of her life into an envelope and held her breath to hear back. That kind of consideration is instilled by growing up with loving, generous parents who put their children at the center of their lives: Briggs and Glenda Leonard.

Chris remembers his parents reading Diane's letter and pushing back from their table in silence. He says that Briggs looked across at his wife and said, "Well, dear, we've had him for more than thirty-five years, haven't we? I guess we're willing to share."

Chris Leonard has to halt for a moment before going on. "That's pretty big, isn't it?"

Karen Leonard threw a surprise party for Chris's fortieth

birthday. What surprise could possibly be left—that Alex had been a baby left in the wreckage of the UFO in Roswell? That might explain the sandy-red beard . . .

Chris walked in, and of course everyone was there. His mother and father. Karen. Justin, Sam, and Kate, his children. Diane. Alex and Meg.

"Everywhere I turned, there were people looking out for me," Chris says.

"MY MOM AND DAD are the most amazing people," he says. "They just want good stuff for me. That's what real parents are, aren't they? I think I can see and appreciate all of the good things that have happened to me *because* I am adopted. It makes me think about some of the things that could have happened, but didn't. If I'd just been born to my mom and dad, they still would have been great parents. But I wouldn't have thought anything of it. I would have thought, 'Well of course, that's just how it happened. No big thing.' But I'm adopted. I know otherwise."

ADOPTIVE PARENTS come to terms early with something every parent has to confront at some turn: our love is not exclusive. Two other people gave our child life, and perhaps a love as powerful as our own. They couldn't keep them. And in the end, no parent can.

All parents have to cheerfully and tearfully accept that their children belong to the world. If we nourish, cherish, and protect them, they will grow up strong enough to mock, challenge, and finally leave us. If we want to keep them in our lives, we've got to have love and memories: nights we hold their heads through fevers and bad dreams, days that we find a beloved fish floating in a bowl and bury him in the park, the long afternoon we spend looking for a lost stuffed toy in the rain. Crying, snarling, protecting, exasperating, hysterics, theatrics, apologies, and laughter make families. Not just blood—mere blood—and genes.

The Pain of What-Ifs, and the Folly of "Don't You Know What?"

PONDERING WHAT-IFS is part of growing up, and it affords mental exercise and refreshment at all ages. I still imagine what it might be like to throw a curveball to pitch the Chicago Cubs into the World Series. I wonder what if I had been born a Dalit (untouchable) in India. Would I have been as wise as a man I once interviewed who collected night soil outside the Calcutta Zoo to make candles? If I had been born a son of King Hussein, would I have worked out peace in the region and snagged Queen Rania besides? If I had been an Illinoisan alive in 1860, would I have voted for Lincoln or Douglas?

But children who are adopted have more palpable alternatives to ponder. Pain may be on some of those paths. At the moment, our daughters don't know a world without a Starbucks nearby, TiVo to stop the action so they can go to the bathroom, and rocky road ice cream in the freezer. I like it that way. A father wants to make his daughters smile and laugh. He wants to keep his children from want, hunger, and hurt. Of course I want them to learn about the world. But I am not eager—in fact, I could wait a zillion years—for them to contemplate how girls who may have been in the cribs next to them will be forced into factories or be exploited by men, while they play soccer and sip hot cocoa with extra sprinkles.

A father whose family had adopted a daughter from Bangladesh once told me, "No matter how hurt or angry your children ever make you—and they will—you must never, never, *never* say, 'Don't you know what we saved you from?' " That's a true obscenity. It is a curse that could discourage the pushing back and outright rebellion that's necessary for children to grow. And while, like most children, ours could stand to treat their mother with more conspicuous gratitude for all she does to dress, bathe, and feed them, and to fill their lives so brilliantly, we don't want a feeling of indebtedness to steer their lives.

Besides: it was they who saved us.

PARENTHOOD IS NUTS and bolts. No, that's carpentry. Parenthood is shit, snot, slime, fear, tears, spit, and spills. It's as intense as combat, which is to say hours of tedium relieved by moments of alarm and flashes of joy to remind you that you're alive. It is intensely practical and profoundly square, even if you're not. It's feeding, wiping, and picking up. Good intentions aren't worthless. But they can't even buy jelly beans for children.

Taber MacCallum grew up in Albuquerque in what he calls a "typically sixties unconventional dysfunctional household," which was not as much fun as it sounds. He says that his mother and father had children, but didn't quite accept that they had become parents, the kind of people who had to feed, diaper, and pick up. They wanted their old lives back, and eventually they divorced. His father philandered, often disappearing to pursue girlfriends at night. Taber thought that his father almost seemed to resent that his son had become the teenager that he could no longer be. Taber was living by his wits, rough and wild, feeling forgotten and forlorn at the age of fourteen.

"I don't think that my mother and father didn't love me," he says. "I'm sure they did. But they weren't bringing groceries into the house. In fact, I was getting the money to buy groceries." Presumably not by selling lemonade.

Taber was an intelligent kid who was doing badly in school and life when a professor named Robert Wall rented a room from his parents for the summer. He and Taber became friendly. Bob recognized qualities in Taber that are manifestly visible now but might have been effectively concealed in a boy edging close to delinquency: intelligence, humor, and, to be sure, loneliness.

At the end of the summer, he asked if Taber would like to come and stay with him and his wife, Vivian Mahlab, in Austin. Taber went for a visit, and essentially came back only to pack. Taber's parents were persuaded, his father rather easily, to let him live with Bob and Vivian. Rather than resent them for their nonchalance, Taber prefers to think that they recognized that their consent was the best thing they could do for their son.

Bob and Vivian became his legal guardians. He stayed with them until college, when they took him on a trip through Europe, then gave him a ticket back to Austin and some traveler's checks. "You're a fine young man," they told him. "Take a month. See the sights. We'll be waiting back home."

"They were *parents*," Taber stresses. "Someone to give you not only unconditional love, but regular meals. Someone to take you to the doctor and dentist. A reason to come home. They were a *miracle*," he says simply. "Two people who told a wild, rambunctious teenager, 'Come live with us, we'll take care of you.' How miraculous an offer is that? Out of the blue, they saved my life."

Taber and his wife, Jane Poynter, are in the life support system business. They are adventurers and explorers who have climbed mountains, sailed oceans, trekked through the outback, and now develop life support systems for space, land, and water research, including the American and Russian space programs (they were married a year after living for two years under the closed dome of Biosphere II, an experience that would lead a lot of people not to speak to each other ever again).

Taber and his birth parents have restored relations. "Why not?" he says. "They're much happier people now. So am I." But before he could explore the heavens and the depths, even Taber MacCallum needed diapers and the practical, hands-on touch of the love of parents.

ADOPTION IS now everywhere. The Evan B. Donaldson Adoption Institute estimates that there are about 1.5 million adopted children in the United States, and that about 60 percent of all Americans know someone who is adopted—next door, down the hall, a cubicle over, a couple of seats away. They are our cousins, sisters, and uncles as well as our children. In some zip codes, adoption has become as common as $3.75 lattes. (A man in the 10023 zip code told me about a playground conversation in which playmates who were born in Korea, Russia, and Kazakhstan and then adopted by New Yorkers asked his son where he was from. "I don't know," said the boy. "Guess I'm from here.")

Adoption is transforming millions of people, not just—or maybe least of all—children. Families are broadening their embrace to include the world. One recent morning after a girls' sleepover, my niece, Juliette, put her arms around Elise and Lina and asked, "We'll be cousins till we die, right?" Right. Our little California blond niece, cousins forever with our Jiangxi Province daughters. Who can say how thousands of those interrelationships may rearrange the way we see the world?

Yet formal, legal adoptions in the United States have been in decline since 1970. Birth control and the legalization of abortion surely have something to do with it. So does our changed morality. Unmarried women who have babies feel less disapproval, and now have more resources, including public encouragement, to hold on to their children and try to be good mothers.

The number one reason most people cite today for exploring adoption is infertility. And it is just another fact of life, if you please, that the assisted fertility industry offers ways to have children that are easier, quicker, and even less expensive than adoption.

Adoptions can now cost more than $25,000 and take years. This rules out more than a few good people, even with the small tax credit provided by the federal government. Some medical plans will reimburse the charges for in vitro fertilization; I know of none that cover the costs of adoption. A few companies will contribute a modest amount toward an adoption by an employee. It's a gracious gesture to say that family is valued. But these contributions are an easy benefit to cut when business is bad.

Age limits in adoption programs rule out other potential parents, even as fertility specialists make childbearing years seem illimitable. We live in a time when couples in their late forties, single women, committed gay couples, or, for that matter, a single woman in her sixties can walk into a fertility clinic and have a child in their arms nine and a half months from the time they pay a fee. They don't have to hurtle and humble themselves through rounds of interviews, finger-prints, spurious assessments, and background checks or years of uncertainty, anxiety, and delay.

Having children has become a business. Formal, legal adoption is still considered a good thing to do. It thus suffers a competitive disadvantage, and I mean to put this in commercial terms. Fertility centers, if not the adoption programs, know they're in competition. Many of them advertise the practical medical advantages of childbirth, such as being able to trace your child's genetic history. This particular claim may be true. But it also dramatically exaggerates how genetic history can predict even eye color, much less a predisposition for cancers, respiratory disorders, or heart disease (which in any case may be closer to being treated by the time a child grows into middle age).

The picture of people paging through donor profiles, almost like paint or fabric swatches in a book, to select a sperm or egg donor by physical features, education, and artistic or mathematical abilities makes me queasy. I am not entitled to any moral disapproval. But it seems to me that discovery is part of the joy of having and loving children. Seeing them develop traits, interests, and talents that we never had, or at least never discovered, is one of the ways in which sons and daughters make us continue to grow after we make the mistake of thinking that we are all grown up. We want our children to be free and strong enough to grow up differently. Maybe those of us who adopt might be in a better position to appreciate this.

I also know that there are deep intangible factors at work. The drive to bear children—to feel a child grow inside and give birth—is profound for many women (I won't attempt any New Age contortions to convince anyone that such an instinct also beats strongly in sensitive men). Medical technologies can assist couples in bringing about this happy result. My wife and I tried. I would never suggest that adoption improves on such a marvel. But bringing children into your life, loving them completely, and committing yourself to their happiness and future is a miracle, too.

I also know that there is exaltation in seeing yourself, and your loved one, in your child's face. There is an instinct to see your children as inheritors and carriers of your family's lineage, history, and traits. Of course it would be wonderful to have children who directly reflect my wife's great wit, graciousness, and beauty. And so we do: our daughters. My wife is revealed in their expressions, their humor, and their laughter. She is visible in all the critical and distinctive little characteristics that we cherish as we fall in love.

I don't recall being presented with a single test to adopt our daughters that was silly, insensitive, excessive, or unwise. But the whole panoply of regulations, examinations, and redundant charges can discourage good prospective parents and drive them to fertility clinics while millions of children who literally hunger for families and are starved for love grow up in institutions or a succession of foster homes.

Adopting a child to prove something is not a healthy motivation. I would seriously consider alerting the authorities if I heard a prospective parent say, "We want to adopt because it's the most environmentally responsible thing to do. Don't want to increase our carbon footprint, after all!"

But I sometimes wonder about people who scold about global warming and the perils of overpopulation and then go through multiple rounds of fertility treatments when there are already millions of children without families. Putting children who need love and care into families who crave the love of a child is one of the great unfinished endeavors of the world. Nothing would do more to increase the amount of love on this planet, which is a kind of global warming that we could all use. I wish that people who want to become parents would consider adoption as a great way to have a family from the start, and not just a last resort.

We Fit

As I said, we know the really hard part is ahead. We look forward to all of the usual challenges of growing up that friends are so eager to warn us about (the extraterrestrial body snatchers who will take the souls of our two winsome girls and insert teenage demons into their flesh) and perhaps a few more.

I know that at some point our daughters will figure out that they were born to Chinese dynastic princesses. They will get angry and ask why we ever plucked them out of rich, burgeoning China to take them into the desperate hurly-burly of the declining urban West. They'll whine to their friends (who will be studying Mandarin in all the best schools), "Can you believe my parents? They took us out of the fastest-growing economy in the world! To drag us to this dead-broke backwater!"

I'm sure I'll be hurt. I don't know what I will say. I hope I'll remember to acknowledge the obvious: Yes, there was something utterly selfish in what we did. We wanted a child. We heard you needed parents. We wanted a miracle in our lives. Darlings, it was you.

WE LIKE TO SPEND a few weeks in the summer in a small village in Brittany where Caroline used to go as a child. We have relatives there. When we're back, we're the family with the glamorous French girl who went to America and came back with a half-Jewish husband and two full-Chinese daughters. Typical American family, we tell them.

One night, we went to a circus. A small family circus that moves from one small town to another over the summer, with two miniature horses, two threadbare llamas, two spitting camels, six little dogs, and four dogged chimps who ride them all while jumping rope.

A Roma family from the Czech Republic ran the circus. The father was the ringmaster, leading the horses, llamas, camels, and dogs around the ring. The mother wore a spangly red suit as she swung from the trapeze and slithered up twisting ropes. A teenage daughter stood tippy-toe and did backflips on the backs of the horses as they cantered in a circle. Their young son—eight, nine years old—was a little clown who took tickets, sold popcorn, and put on a red ringmaster's jacket himself for the last act. With his small face still sooty from his clown's cosmetic stubble, he announced, "The circus will live as long as there are children."

PETA and the child welfare authorities would never permit this circus in America. But we loved it. The animals seemed well cared for. The little boy looked happy and healthy, and was learning about the world.

And we found the circus family to be an irresistible little reflection of our own. The graceful mother with her death-defying swings, the blurred line between animal and human relatives, and the little boy blaring, "Ladies and gentlemen and children of all ages! And now . . ."

Elise had just started saying that. She'd pull on one of her ballet costumes, snap Lina into a pink princess dress, dangle a ribbon in front of our cat's nose to lead them all into the living room, and announce, "Ladies and gentleman! And now, our cat, Nana, will . . . run after this ribbon!"

Our cousin Camille was with us. Our daughters scrambled onto her lap, whispered breathless, cunning little requests for popcorn, and smoothed the scarf that she was wearing over her smooth head.

Camille, at twenty-one, was dying from the cancer she had battled for several months. She was a French girl with American moxie. She wanted to see London, Washington, Chicago, Las Vegas, and New York. She was bold, striking, kind, and funny. She wanted to finish school in small-town France and come to America, where she believed people could become whatever they wanted to be. We were going to help her. Elise wanted a bunk bed so that Camille could come to America and sleep above her. We wanted that, too.

Camille had always been drawn to our daughters. She loved their *difference,* their assertiveness and spirit. When they sat in her lap, they seemed to draw calm from her while she breathed in their spunkiness. When she'd come to our place after a round of cancer treatments—nasty, nauseating treatments—I think she treasured their fits of pique and crankiness as vital signs of life. Camille may have been too tired to complain. Our girls lent her their voices.

I caught sight of Camille and our daughters during intermission at the circus that night. Fearlessly they held out their hands for a camel's kisses. It was a night to cherish and marvel at how sometimes the earth spins to let three fierce and funny souls from different places on earth find each other.

A few months later, my wife and daughters were able to spend one of the last days of Camille's life with her in her apartment in the center of town. There was little doubt that this would be the last time they would see each other, but Caroline says that the day was truly blissful. The cancer had clawed into Camille's bones and brain; she was profoundly tired. So they all curled up on her bed in the afternoon sunlight and spread out a map of where we live. Lina dozed. Caroline and Elise showed Camille the river that runs by our apartment, Elise's school, their favorite cupcake shop around the corner, and all of the most fun places they would take her.

It was a show, of course. But I am from a family of troupers who believe in the power of good shows to divert and enchant. My wife and Camille both knew by then that she would never be able to join us. But I think that when you know in your bones and heart that you may have only a little left of life's blessing, you want to spend it in hope, not despair. Hope is what you want to share with the children around you.

Camille died a few days later. Our daughter's hearts bear the first real cracks they have had to endure since we came into each other's lives. Our girls had a lot of laughs to give Camille in the years ahead; she had a lot of love for them. But I think that some lives are like diamonds. They pack a lot of light and brilliance into a small space. I remember seeing the three of them stick out their little pink tongues as the camel slurped water with his huge rubber band of a tongue. The girls giggled together and I thought, "Oh my God. They've adopted each other."

I APPRECIATE the majesty of the universe, even as I do not understand it. I have wildly inconsistent ideas about God and religion. Because I want our girls to know that they can tell me the truth, whatever it is, and should expect it from me, I cannot bring myself to tell them that Camille, or my father, or our beloved fish Salman Fishdie (we are on Sammi IV at this writing) watches over us in heaven and someday I'll be there, too. I cannot tell them why a just God would let millions of little children suffer while a scintilla of others are swept to survival and comfort across the ocean.

Call if you know the answer; our operators are standing by.

Yet we all devoutly believe in the Tooth Fairy. When our girls lose a tooth, she wafts in through our balcony door, gently slips a coin and a candy beneath their pillow, and drinks a glass of pomegranate juice, thoughtfully leaving a wash of pink at the bottom of the glass to substantiate her visit.

Those of us who have been adopted, or have adopted or want to adopt children, must believe in a world in which the tumblers of the universe can click in unfathomable ways that deliver strangers into our lives. The tectonic plates shift, the radiation belt springs a small hole, and children from the other side of the world, or the other side of the street, can wind up feeling utterly right in our arms.

ONE NIGHT in Brittany, some relatives and friends decided to set off fireworks along the beach. Camille had just had a round of chemotherapy and went to bed. The sun doesn't set until ten during summer in the northern climes, and ordinarily Elise would have gone to bed, too. But hearing her older cousins rave about all the twizzlers, firecrackers, and Roman candles they were about to light only made her ornery and determined to stay up; and what Elise wants, so does Lina.

Their older cousins romped down to a clearing along the beach. A couple of uncles helped them light the long string fuses. By the time the fifth and sixth Roman candles had burst in the sky, Lina was already drowsing on Caroline's shoulder, and Elise was beginning to fade. I opened my arms. Elise turned around to climb into my embrace. She knew exactly where her knees would fit on top of my thighs, where her hands could wrap around my neck, where her head could rest along my shoulder. I slid one arm beneath my daughter, flattened the palm of my other hand on her back, and squeezed lightly: our signal that I had her, all was well, we're all here, we're all safe, you can drift off now. You can be sure of us.

My wife's deep brown eyes were alight. I felt Elise exhale lightly across my ear, and I clutched her just a little more tightly. I whispered to all of us the very first words that came to me when I decided to try to tell our story: "Baby, we were meant for each other."

Acknowledgments

FIRST AND LAST: my thanks to all the people mentioned herein who opened their lives to me—and now to you.

Also to Susan Alvarado, Han Feng, Mary Glendinning, Jennifer Hershey, Kee Malesky, Adam Pertman, Kelly Straw, and Ed Victor. All mistakes are mine.

This book is dedicated to my wife, Caroline Richard. So is my life.

I don't have a talent that is adequate to return a favor to skilled neurosurgeons. But I hope that Dr. Edward Benzel, Dr. Neil Cherian, Ann Henwood, and the rest of the staff at the remarkable Cleveland Clinic will accept our family's thanks for giving me a new lease on life, and filling an anxious time with caring, laughter, and warmth.

Every year, the five families who all had children put into our arms at the same time at the adoption center in Nanchang get together for a weekend. At a recent reunion, the older girls ran off into Elise's bedroom. We heard giggling, rustling, and lots more giggling. Elise finally emerged to instruct the adults, "Look at here, everybody. And now, you will see something very beautiful." We sure did. Our girls came clip-clopping into the living room in crinkly gowns and plastic heels taken from Elise's ample store of costumes. Their younger brothers and sister joined us to clap and laugh.

This book is also for Clara June, Elise, Elizabeth, Jasmine, Polly, Daniel, Lina, Wade, Leighton, and Lucy. You gave us new lives. You will rock the world.

About the Author

SCOTT SIMON is the host of NPR's *Weekend Edition with Scott Simon*. He has reported stories from all fifty states and every continent, covered ten wars from El Salvador to Iraq, and won every major award in broadcasting. He also hosts shows for PBS and appears on BBC TV. He is the author of the novels *Windy City* and *Pretty Birds*, the memoir *Home and Away*, and of *Jackie Robinson and the Integration of Baseball*. He lives with his wife, Caroline, and their daughters, Elise and Paulina.

www.scottsimonbooks.com